SHARING CHRIST
When You Feel You Can't

SHARING CHRIST

When You Feel You Can't

*Making it easier to tell your friends
and family about your faith in Christ*

Daniel Owens

with Perry Brown

CROSSWAY BOOKS • WHEATON, ILLINOIS
A DIVISION OF GOOD NEWS PUBLISHERS

Sharing Christ When You Feel You Can't

Copyright © 1997 by Daniel Owens

Published by Crossway Books,
a division of Good News Publishers
1300 Crescent Street
Wheaton, Illinois 60187.

Cover design: Dennis Hill

First printing, 1997

Printed in the United States of America

Library of Congress Cataloging-in-Publication Data
Owens, Daniel, 1956-
    Sharing Christ when you feel you can't : making it easier to tell
your friends and family about your faith in Christ / Daniel Owens.
      p.   cm.
    ISBN 0-89107-935-1
    1. Witness bearing (Christianity)   2. Family—Religious life.
I. Title.
BV4520.094   1997
248'.5—dc21   96-52236

05	04	03	02	01	00	99	98						
15	14	13	12	11	10	9	8	7	6	5	4	3	2

Dedicated to my wife, Debby,
who has lived out Proverbs 18:24—to have friends,
you must show that you're friendly—
and to Ben, Jordan, and Taylor

CONTENTS

FOREWORD

By Luis Palau

POLITICAL POLLSTERS WOULD CALL ROBIN A "SOCCER MOM." SHE lives in a middle-class suburb north of Chicago. She's married, has two young children, and faithfully attends Sunday school, worship services, and a women's Bible study at her church.

The summer before the *Say Yes Chicago* evangelistic crusade, Robin met Patricia, a young woman in her neighborhood, while walking her dog. The two women continued to run into each other occasionally, and Robin began to wonder if Patricia attended church. *Maybe she'd like to come to a Bible study with me*, Robin thought.

But the weeks passed, the kids started another busy school year, and Robin lost touch with Patricia. Then at a pre-crusade training seminar designed to encourage Christians to build relationships with unchurched friends, Robin thought of Patricia. She wrote Patricia's name on her prayer card, promising to pray for her and invite her to an upcoming evangelistic event. The problem was, she had forgotten Patricia's last name and had lost her phone number. Robin was praying for Patricia nearly every day, but without a phone number it was too easy to put off inviting her to the crusade.

This book is written for Robin—and, would you believe, for a crusade evangelism veteran like me. I wholeheartedly believe in one-on-one evangelism. I practice it and teach it. But given the choice of boarding a plane for Hong Kong to proclaim the Gospel of Jesus Christ to 30,000 people in a stadium or crossing the street to start up a conversation with my neighbors about spiritual things, it's sometimes easier to hop on the Boeing 747.

It's not easy to talk about Jesus Christ with a neighbor or friend. This despite a ton of evidence that most Americans are more than willing to talk about spiritual things. Thanks to a host of best sellers, everybody's talking about angels and near-death experiences. Year after year Gallup polls show that almost everyone believes there's life after death. *Newsweek* ran a story titled "The Art of Dying Well." Most Americans believe there's life after death, the article said, yet they live in terror of death. "Clinicians can only tell us what happens to the body when death occurs. But at the moment of death what matters is what happens to *me*." People want to know how to get to heaven.

Following an evangelistic women's luncheon, a woman thanked me for presenting the Gospel. "I've gone to church almost every Sunday my whole life, but I never felt what happened here today," she said. "Often after church I would stand outside and say to myself, *But nothing happened . . . nothing happened.* Today it happened."

Here was a God-fearing woman, searching for years to know God and now looking for the words to express the joy she felt the moment she invited Christ into her life. She just needed to know how. Someone had to build a bridge to her life and bring her to the luncheon to hear the Gospel.

We know, of course, that God loves all people and desires a relationship with each of us. He already has provided the way. His Son died on the cross, and the Holy Spirit convicts of sin. But the amazing thing we must never forget is that God's plan is to work through you and me to bring others into His kingdom. We are His witnesses.

That responsibility need not fill us with fear. My good friend Dan Owens has helped thousands of Christians begin to share their faith, not through how-to's and methods (as helpful as they are), but by simply caring, sharing, and listening in everyday situations.

Just days before the *Say Yes Chicago* crusade, Robin got serious about finding Patricia's phone number and finally made the call. "She was excited about coming," Robin says. "Why did I make it so difficult?" Riding with Robin to the crusade rally Friday night, Patricia said, "I'm not going forward or anything like that." Surprised that Patricia was even thinking about it, Robin put her friend at ease. "Let's just go and have a good time."

At the invitation, however, Patricia said to Robin, "I want to go down, but I'm not going by myself." Robin accompanied her friend and prayed with her when she invited Christ into her life.

Robin put into words why you'll want to read this book and share your faith as often as possible: "You have so much joy in your heart when you can be used by the Lord to bring somebody to Him!"

To be leading people into God's eternal kingdom—nothing brings greater joy and satisfaction. May that be your experience!

1

What's Holding You Back?

I REMEMBER ONE OF THE FIRST TIMES I SHARED MY FAITH WITH someone. I was a fairly new Christian attending Liberty University, a Christian college in Virginia. As a member of the football team, I was required to go door to door witnessing (a prerequisite for anyone who wanted to play sports).

One Saturday I went door to door with Randy, a pastor's son and a junior in college who had done this sort of thing many times before. By the time we reached the fourth house Randy turned to me and said, "Okay, Dan, the next one is yours."

I was so scared, I tried to refuse; but Randy insisted. We walked to the house and knocked on the door. When an elderly woman opened the door, I began my speech, telling her that we were going from house to house to talk to people about the Lord. When she heard that, to my surprise and fright, she invited us in, sat us down, and brought her husband to us.

To this day I don't know what I said. All I know is, when I finished I asked, "Would you like to open your heart to Christ?" To my shock, the elderly man said yes, so we prayed together.

As we were leaving, the woman pulled me aside, put her arm

around me, and said, "I've been praying for years for my husband to come to Jesus, but he's had no interest whatsoever. Today you came by and led my husband to Jesus Christ. Thank you!"

I'll never forget that experience. Of course, Randy was a bit shocked and even impressed that the Lord used me, but no more than I was. If it hadn't been for Randy's persistence, I would have missed out on leading someone to the Lord—solely because of fear.

Afraid to Evangelize

Why is sharing our faith so difficult? What makes it so hard to give our testimony to somebody, to quote a few Bible verses to him or her?

What scares many people is the idea that we have to go down on the street corner, confront someone with a Gospel presentation, and keep prompting her until he or she prays the sinner's prayer.

Confrontational evangelism works for some people, but most of us are relational. That's why I like to do what I call *conversational evangelism*—establishing friendships, developing relationships with others, building bridges into other people's lives.

Still, we're all generally cowards when it comes to sharing our faith, even with those we know. I consider myself the Number One Chicken. Why are we afraid? Five reasons come to mind.

Fear of Failure

We are afraid we will fail. So often we think, *What if I share my faith with someone and he doesn't respond? What if I lead someone to the point of receiving Jesus Christ, but she rejects the invitation?*

After becoming a Christian at age seventeen, I was trained in evangelism. I was taught that believers confront people, lead them to the point of receiving Christ, and then pray with them to accept the Lord. I put upon myself the responsibility of saving every person I saw. I ended up feeling an incredible burden to witness to the person I sat next to on an airplane, to the waitress that served me in a restaurant, to everyone with whom I came in contact. With this feeling of responsibility came the fear that I would fail. I began to notice that I was retreating from people because I didn't want the burden. Thankfully, I finally learned that God hasn't made us responsible for the salvation of everyone with whom we come into contact.

Look at Acts 1:8—"But you will receive power when the Holy Spirit comes on you; and you will be my witnesses in Jerusalem, and in all Judea and Samaria, and to the ends of the earth." Jesus didn't say, "I want you to lead everyone you come in contact with to Me." Rather, all God is asking us to do is to be His witness wherever we go. We are a light to the world, and we speak on His behalf.

It's not our responsibility to convict people of sin and to get them to drop to their knees and open their hearts to Jesus Christ. Only the Holy Spirit can bring conviction and transformation. If that's His responsibility, then you and I aren't failures if those we talk to aren't ready to respond to the invitation to trust Christ.

We often make witnessing, the sharing of our faith, more difficult than it needs to be. It's time we stopped putting pressure on ourselves, thinking we must lead some person to Christ. Instead, we should relax and let the Holy Spirit work through us, asking, "To whom do You want me to be a light? To whom do You want me to witness?" and leave the results up to the Lord.

Fear of Rejection

We also hesitate to build bridges to others because *we are afraid we will be rejected.*

Often when we share our faith, we feel that people see us as strange ducks or fanatics or something equally odd. Non-Christians might even find avoid us because we are "religious."

I know I often have been given that "I'll humor him" look when I talk about the Lord. People respond with a half-hearted, "Oh, really? Interesting." Then they walk the other way the next time they see me coming. They tell their colleagues, "You know Owens? That guy is a religious fanatic."

No one likes to be rejected. It's not a pleasant experience. I've never met anyone who wakes up in the morning, looks in the mirror, and says, "Today I want to be rejected." We want people to love us, to accept us, to welcome us. But the Bible tells us that we're likely to experience rejection.

Jesus tells us, "If the world hates you, keep in mind that it hated me first" (John 15:18). We know that fact intellectually, but emotionally, being rejected is painful, so we sometimes decline to build relationship bridges with others.

Fear of Contamination

The third reason we hesitate to share our faith with others is that *we are afraid we will be contaminated.* We are afraid to meet our unsaved friends and relatives on their turf because we think their sinful activities and attitudes will taint us.

We want them to come over to our side instead. We want them to attend our churches and our Bible studies because we don't feel comfortable going where they are. We don't want to become defiled, so we retreat.

But Jesus did not ask us to be spiritual hermits, to lock ourselves up in some monastery or nunnery. He asked us to be "in the world" (see John 17:11). Jesus prayed this for His disciples: "My prayer is not that you take them out of the world but that you protect them from the evil one" (John 17:15). Earlier in His ministry Jesus said that we are to be a "light" to the world (Matthew 5:14-16).

My oldest son attends a public school. During a parent/teacher conference one of his teachers, a Christian, told my wife and me, "I want you to know that your son shines bright." I was so proud of him.

Most of us like to surround ourselves with Christians because we are comfortable with people of like mind and like faith. We see them at church, we invite them into our homes, we associate with them at work. How easy it is to evade Jesus' command to go out into the world and shine so others will believe in Him. It's hard to be a light to the world when we're always hanging around other lamps. You have to go into the darkness to shine.

Lack of Skill

The fourth reason we hesitate to build a bridge to others is that *we are afraid we just don't have the skill for it.*

Not many of us have gone to seminary or have received formal biblical training. Because we think we don't know much about the Bible, we're often afraid to open our mouths and tell people about Jesus. We think, *If someone asks me a question to which I don't know the answer, how will I respond? I won't know what to say.*

Bible knowledge is good, but God doesn't require a degree in theology before He can use you to witness to others. Many of Jesus' own disciples had limited educations, yet ended up being the leaders of the church.

The apostles Peter and John are prime examples. In Acts 4:13 we read that after they had shared the Gospel before the Sanhedrin, the rulers, elders, and teachers of the law were "astonished" because Peter and John were "unschooled, ordinary men."

What made the difference? Peter and John "had been with Jesus." God didn't care how much they knew or how much training they had. It was enough that they had been with Jesus. Can that be said of us? Are we spending so much time with the Savior that it shows?

If we spend time with Jesus, we can do incredible things as He works through us. Reading our Bibles, praying, and meditating on the things of God are essential if we want to share our faith effectively. Conversely, it's almost impossible to build bridges to people if we're not walking with the Lord. If we're not spending time with God, we won't have a growing love for Him and as a result won't have a love for people.

Another reason God could use Peter and John was because they were empowered by His Spirit—the same Spirit who lives in each and every believer.

What a relief this is! No matter how unschooled or ordinary I am, no matter what my age or education is, God can use me. And if someone asks me a tough question, I can trust His Holy Spirit, who lives inside me, to give me just the right words to say.

In fact, I've found that God doesn't use the person who thinks, *I've got degrees. I'm brilliant. I'm a great communicator. I can do this.* If we think that way, we're going to fall on our face in defeat. I've seen God use primary-age children, teenagers, uneducated adults—*anyone who is willing.* God uses the person who is humble, who says, "Lord, I don't know a lot. I'm not a great orator. But here I am. Use me."

Consider the story of the blind man whom Jesus healed during His ministry on earth. When the Pharisees, the religious leaders of the day, began to investigate the blind man's healing, they claimed that Jesus could not be from God because He healed someone on the Sabbath. They began to question the man who had been blind about what had happened. He responded that he didn't know who Jesus was, then said, "One thing I do know. I was blind but now I see!" (John 9:25).

The Pharisees had a great knowledge of God's Word. They had investigated and studied and meditated on the Scriptures. But they knew less about Jesus than the unschooled blind man who dismissed their questions in one statement. He knew what had happened to him, and all the objections or doubts that others had were not going to change that fact.

Salvation stories are a powerful tool. God can greatly use you, not because of your incredible knowledge of the Bible, but because of your testimony. You can say, "I may not know all about the Bible or have all the answers, but this one thing I do know: God changed my life, and I'm no longer the person I once was." (I'll say more on writing out your testimony in a later chapter.)

Thank God that we don't have to wait until we know everything before we begin to build bridges to others. Since we have seen the power of Jesus in our lives and the Holy Spirit resides in us, we can reach out to others.

Not Seeing the Need

The final reason we hesitate to share our faith with others is that *we don't see the need.*

A pastor of a thousand-plus member church told me recently, "Dan, this church is in trouble right now because none of my staff or elders, myself included, have a burden for evangelism."

I was surprised, so I asked, "You have no outreach at all going on in your church?"

"No," he replied. "We just take care of the sheep here." That's sad and frightening, but not unusual.

Before a recent evangelistic crusade, one of my colleagues at the Luis Palau Evangelistic Association gave a presentation in a church to more than 2,000 people attending the two morning worship services that Sunday. He explained the upcoming opportunity to share the Gospel with relatives, friends, and neighbors. Then he asked them to take the friendship evangelism prayer card from their bulletin and write down the names of five people for whom they would pray and whom they would seek to invite to an evangelistic event. In this well-known evangelical church that was generally supportive of the crusade, only one person turned in the response portion of the friendship evangelism card. Only one out of more than 2,000 people made a commitment to pray for unsaved friends and neighbors!

We have become so preoccupied with our own lives, our own Christian world, that we forget we meet people every day who are suffering, who are without hope, who are desperate to hear that Someone loves them, and who are going to spend eternity in hell unless something happens.

Whether preacher or parishioner, we must keep a careful vigil against becoming so preoccupied that we forget that other people truly need the Lord. We may be teaching children's church, leading the youth choir, hosting a Bible study. That's good. But what are we doing to reach out to those people who need to hear the message of salvation? We can't get so caught up in doing good things that we ignore the Great Commission.

"Don't Just Sit There—Do Something!"

When I served as an associate pastor in California, I finally came to the realization that people were not coming to the church, knocking on the door on Sunday morning, and saying, "Can someone tell me about Jesus? I want to learn how I can get to heaven."

We can't wait for people to come to us. When we study the life of Jesus, we see Him spending more time in the marketplace and homes than He ever did in the synagogue. Jesus went where the people were.

In Matthew 9 we see Jesus eating dinner with the sinners and the tax collectors. When the religious leaders of the day saw this, they became angry and questioned Jesus' disciples. When Jesus heard their question, He said, "It is not the healthy who need a doctor, but the sick. But go and learn what this means: 'I desire mercy, not sacrifice. For I have not come to call the righteous, but sinners'" (Matthew 9:12-13).

Jesus' strategy was to bring His message to those who most needed it—sinners. That should be our approach as well.

Improper Motivations

If you're anything like me, you have missed opportunities to share Jesus Christ with other people because you're preoccupied or fears have crept into your heart. Thinking about what we haven't done for the Lord can fill us with guilt and place undue pressure on us.

But God doesn't want us to feel guilty and uptight about evangelism. In fact, the pressure we put on ourselves to share Christ with others may distort true motivations for evangelism.

When I became a Christian at age seventeen, I was told immediately of my responsibility to share my faith. And I was given many opportunities to do just that. As I look back over my life, however, my motivations for giving out the Gospel often were not proper. You may have detected these improper motives in your life as well.

First is the motivation of *trying to win God's approval.* I felt for many years that God would love me more if I shared my faith in Jesus Christ with other people. I thought I would earn God's highest rating, His four-star commendation, if I got out and shared my faith.

Have you ever felt that way? It's good to know there's nothing we can do to make God love us more than He does already, and there's also nothing we can do to make God love us less. He's not impressed by the things we do or don't do. What an eye-opener to realize that sharing our faith is not a way of getting God to love us more—He already loves us fully.

The second improper motivation for sharing our faith is *pride.* Many Christians think, *If I share Christ with someone, I'll be a "super Christian."*

I've been guilty of this myself. I remember being at small-group Bible studies where people were sharing what God had done in their lives that past week. When my turn came around I would say something like, "Pray for me because I shared Christ with a fellow at work this week." The need for prayer was the last thing on my mind. I really just wanted to impress the other Christians with how great a Christian I was.

Most of us have experienced the awed hush that comes over a room of believers when someone tells about sharing his faith with a coworker or a waitress in a restaurant or a seatmate on an airplane. Everyone is amazed, as though anyone who witnesses for God is somebody special. Because it seems that so few of us share our faith, we think anyone who does it is on a higher spiritual level.

It's easy to develop a sense of pride when we think we are one of the "few" true friendship evangelists, a rare breed—a truly committed Christian. Although we may not voice our thoughts, we may begin to think, *Others may not evangelize—they're not good Christians. But I have a strong faith. I talk to people about Jesus.*

Disaster is just around the corner when pride is our motive.

The third improper motivation for sharing our faith is thinking that *God needs "famous" people to speak out for Him, so we shouldn't bother with ordinary folk.* This attitude assumes that God just isn't as concerned about the average people we meet day by day.

With the hero mentality so prevalent in our culture, many of us fall into this trap. We begin to plan our hit list of people who, if they came to know the Lord, would do great things for Him. Instead of listening to God and sharing the Gospel with those whom God puts in our path, we follow our own plan—ignoring the John and Jane Does we know and praying, occasionally, for celebrities who could accomplish so much for God.

Why do you and I want to share Jesus Christ with other people? What is our motivation for wanting to share our faith with others? Is it because we feel guilty? Because we don't want other believers to think we're weak Christians? Because we want to win God's approval? Because we like feeling "spiritual" or proud of ourselves?

Proper Motivations

Many times we do have improper motivation for wanting to evangelize others. But God can change our hearts and help us have the proper motives for sharing our faith.

We should be motivated to reach out to others, first and foremost, because *we love the Lord and want to be obedient to Him.*

I'll be honest. At times I don't feel like sharing my faith. I've been in several dozen countries to preach the Gospel, and sometimes I don't want to be there. I don't like the country, I don't like the terrain, I don't like the food, and I don't have a great love for the people. I should, but sometimes I don't. But I'm there because God called me to go. I give out the Gospel because I love the Lord and want to be obedient.

Our second motivation should be that we have *a heart of love, a heart of compassion.* We should be so concerned about people that we want to demonstrate God's love to them.

My wife, Debby, developed a friendship with a seventy-five-year-old man who lives in Germany. He visits the United States twice a year to see his son, who lives in the house across from ours.

One day Debby saw this elderly man, alone at home, watching our two boys playing. She wrapped a plate of cookies, took it over to him, and introduced herself. He couldn't believe someone would do something like that for him. Although he didn't realize it at the time, Debby's actions demonstrated the love that God has for him.

Possibilities for building bridges exist all around us if we are willing to conquer our fears and allow a love for God and a love for people to flow through us.

"I love the Lord, but I've always been afraid to step out and say something," said a San Fernando Valley resident, Linda, who had just experienced for the first time the joy of introducing someone to Jesus Christ. "Now that I've started, don't ever hold me back."

2

This Is An Emergency!

WHEN THE NORTHRIDGE EARTHQUAKE ROCKED CALIFORNIA'S SAN Fernando Valley on January 17, 1994, I was right in the middle of it. In fact, I'm pretty sure my hotel room was the epicenter.

I awoke at 4:32 that morning as the TV and I crossed paths in mid-air. I stumbled out of the room, bumping into furniture and dodging shattered glass. Following emergency exit signs, I raced down three flights of stairs—watching as huge cracks split the walls. I had no doubt I was going to die.

The earthquake ended just as I burst from the building, panting to catch my breath. The emergency exit had deposited me behind the hotel, and the door slammed shut. Surrounded by inky blackness, I realized I had nothing with me—no clothing, no keys.

After sheepishly recovering my belongings, I joined thousands of residents fleeing for safety—in my case, to the nearest airport for my scheduled flight north. Within hours, as news of the devastating 6.8 quake spread across the nation, Americans gathered food, blankets, and clothes to send to those who needed assistance. Relief agencies deployed personnel to Southern California.

Urgency was required to meet the physical needs of those who survived the Northridge quake. In the same way, people all around us are facing spiritual disasters and need urgent care.

Loneliness, hopelessness, anger, guilt, and related problems burden many of our spiritually lost friends, neighbors, and coworkers. Their homes are being ripped apart by abuse, their marriages are being shaken by infidelity, their children are being destroyed by lies. People are starving from a lack of spiritual food and are searching for help.

Time to Wake Up!

As believers, we need to wake up to the urgency of our task. Jesus tells us, "The Son of Man came to seek and to save what was lost" (Luke 19:10). Though the work of providing salvation is His alone, we need to work as He did to save the lost. We need to work through spiritual relief agencies and come to the aid of those who are still under the wrath of God.

Oswald Chambers defines being lost as "not being where we should be." That's exactly the situation an unsaved person is in. The spiritually lost are not in a right relationship with God. They have never heard that God wants to be their Father and give them an eternal home in heaven. Until they hear and respond to God's invitation to join His family, they will remain lost.

Have you ever been on an outing and gotten lost? The first time I took my girlfriend—now my wife—out on a date, I became disoriented and lost my way on the drive back to her house.

I still remember the feelings that assailed me. I knew her father would run me through the wringer for bringing his daughter home late, and I was sure he would break my nose. He wouldn't believe the old line, "We got lost"—even though in this case it was true!

Perspiration gathered on my brow and palms and around my collar. I was confused, angry, and restless. I knew where I wanted to go and where I needed to be, but I wasn't sure how to get there.

That's how people without Jesus Christ feel—lost and confused. I was talking with a sixty-one-year-old British man, and he told me, "Dan, there's something I don't understand. I'm retiring. I have several houses and cars. I'm financially secure. I have a beautiful family. I have all the trappings of the world. But something is not right in my life. I feel restless. I'm not content."

Why was he unhappy? Because he was spiritually lost. Nothing could ever completely satisfy him because he was not where he should be—in a right relationship with God. Augustine, an early church father, wrote, "Our hearts are restless, O God, until we find rest in Thee." Thankfully, that day the Brit opened his heart to Jesus Christ and found rest.

Many people today are spiritually lost, feeling restless and discontented, and are unsure why they feel that way. But in the theological sophistication of the late twentieth century many dismiss the lost condition of humanity, denying that people without Jesus Christ are separated from God for eternity. Many others believe in universalism, the view that Jesus will forgive everyone in the end and take them to heaven. Even born-again Christians demonstrate this kind of belief—by their inaction. Only what we truly believe moves us to action.

It is imperative that we realize that the spiritually lost will continue to wander through life, searching futilely for the way to true satisfaction and happiness unless they are shown the way to a right relationship with God. We must recognize these things to be absolutely true, then reach out lovingly with the truth.

A Passion for the Lost

Before we can build bridges of relationship to those we know who need Jesus Christ, it's important that we gain a passion for them.

Have you ever lost something valuable? While on a trip overseas, I called home to catch up on the news. As I talked to my wife on the phone, I knew I didn't have her full attention. She sounded distracted. Finally I asked her, "What's bothering you?"

She told me, "I've lost the checkbook. It's been missing for two days now." She began to cry as she told me how she had gone back to every store and shop she had visited in the past forty-eight hours and how our two boys helped her tear the house apart trying to find the checkbook. I was amazed at how many stores she had to revisit.

As I listened to her, I realized how utterly frustrated she was. She was searching desperately to find what had become an item of utmost importance.

When we lose something of value, we're never at peace until we find it. The search consumes us; we can't rest until we locate the missing item.

A Picture of God's Heart

That's how God feels about those of His creation who are lost. We see a picture of His heart for the lost in Luke 15. The three parables Jesus tells in that chapter deal with lost things. A shepherd loses a sheep, a woman loses a coin, and a son leaves home and is lost to his father. In each of these stories, the person who lost the item searches diligently and persistently until he finds what he has lost. Then, after he finds it, he calls his friends and neighbors and invites them to rejoice with him. (In the parable of the prodigal son, the father doesn't literally go on a search and rescue mission, but he does yearn for his son's restoration; and when the son returns home, the father is waiting with open arms and a forgiving heart. Though he had remained home in body, he had been searching passionately for his son with his heart.)

Jesus used these three parables to demonstrate how He and His Father feel about those who have spurned His love. He described His journey to earth as a rescue mission: "For the Son of man came to seek and to save what was lost" (Luke 19:10). God diligently searches for the lost of His creation. He doesn't think, *Only one person has wandered away. I have all these others here who already love and appreciate me. I'm not going to waste My time on just one lost person.*

He never stops seeking until He finds that lost one. He says, "How can I rest? How can I stop searching when there are people all over the world who need My Son, Jesus Christ?" And when one person is found, when one sinner repents, the Bible says, "There is rejoicing in the presence of the angels of God" (Luke 15:10).

God does not want any of His creation to be lost to Him. The Bible tells us that God "wants all men to be saved and to come to a knowledge of the truth" (1 Timothy 2:4), and "He is patient . . . not wanting anyone to perish, but everyone to come to repentance" (2 Peter 3:9). God doesn't go a day without thinking about His lost children.

A Parent's Example

In the movie *Home Alone 2*, eleven-year-old Kevin is lost in New York City. His mother has filed a missing person report with the police, but she can't just sit in her hotel room waiting. So she hits the streets, a photo of Kevin in her hand, asking one stranger after another if they've seen her son.

Approaching a police car, she says, "Have you seen my son? He's been missing for two days."

"Have you filed a report, ma'am?" the policeman asks.

"Yes, of course we have."

"Then trust us. We'll handle it."

"Oh . . . I'm his mother."

"I realize that, ma'am, but you're looking for a needle in a haystack."

"Do you have kids?"

"Yes, ma'am."

"And what would you do if one of them was missing?"

"I'd probably be doing the same thing you're doing."

I have often thought what it would be like if one of my three sons were abducted. It's a terrible thought, but picture it for a moment.

I would do everything possible to get my son back. I would notify the authorities, my friends, and anyone who would help with an all-out search for my little one. I would post pictures of him on grocery bags and on the side of milk cartons. I would spend hours upon hours waiting and watching for his return. And when I received the call that my son was found, I would be so excited I wouldn't be able to sit down until he got back to our house, back where he belonged. I would call everyone and shout, "My son has been found!" I would hug him so long and hard that he probably would get tired of it. And then I wouldn't want to let him out of my sight.

Like a parent, God has posted a picture of His lost children in the Bible. Oh, He hasn't given us names or photographs, but He has described their condition and spiritual predicament. God has notified us of the need the lost have and has asked us to help Him in the all-important search. He asks us to watch and wait with

Him, to love His children as He does. And when one of the lost is found, we are invited to rejoice with Him.

Have we developed a heart for the lost? Has God's heart become our heart? I know for myself it's easy to get distracted, to get busy and not see people through God's eyes.

"What Do You See?"

D.L. Moody, America's foremost evangelist during the nineteenth century, preached the Gospel with equal success in London and other cities of Great Britain 120 years ago. Some clergymen, jealous of this uneducated Yankee, desired to know his secret. So they knocked on the door of his hotel room, the story is told, and greeted him by saying, "Mr. Moody, we would like to have a word with you. You come here to London, you have a sixth-grade education, you speak horrible English, your sermons are terribly simple, and yet thousands of people are converted. We want to know, how do you do it?"

Moody invited his guests into his room and walked over to a window. "Tell me," he said, "what do you see?"

One gentleman looked out and said, "I see a park and some children playing."

"Anything else?" Moody asked.

"No, that is basically it."

Another man said, "I see about the same thing except there is an older couple walking hand in hand, enjoying the evening."

A third clergyman added that he saw a young couple, then asked, "Mr. Moody, what do you see?"

As Moody stood there staring out the window, tears began to roll down his cheeks onto his gray beard. "Mr. Moody, what are you looking at?" one of his curious guests asked. "What do you see?"

"When I look out the window, I see countless thousands of souls that will one day spend eternity in hell if they do not find the Savior," Moody said.

That was his secret. Moody had compassion for those who did not know Jesus Christ, and that compassion governed his life. He gave himself to rescuing people from hell.

Do you ever stop and view people like Moody did? Do you ever look compassionately at those whose paths cross yours while you're at school or at work, as you're shopping at the mall, as you're teeing up on the ninth hole? Has the thought ever crossed your mind that the person who bags your groceries and the mechanic who works on your car might be lost? What do you see?

Develop a Love for the Lost

When I came to the Lord, I desired to love the world like God does. But I soon realized that you can't create a love for people on your own. It's easy to get worked up about the condition of the unsaved and feel love for them—until we get on the freeway and some car cuts us off. Then our love for the lost flies out the door as we shake our fist at the unskilled driver.

A love for the lost has to come from God. We can't fake it or create it. I remember wrapping my arms around a globe we used to have in our house and praying, "God, give me a love for the lost. I want to have a love like Yours for the world."

Evangelism is a normal expression of our Christian faith. So if a desire to witness is lacking, we need to cultivate our relationship with God.

Have you ever tried to share Christ with someone when absolutely nothing is happening in your spiritual life? I was sitting on a plane one time talking with a fellow passenger, and the perfect opportunity arose to talk about the Lord. But I had nothing to share because my life right then was so dead spiritually.

Psalm 63:8 (KJV) says, "My soul followeth hard after thee." This implies an intense desire to know God, which is what we need if we are going to be effective in our witness for Christ. Knowing God takes strenuous exertion or discipline. Spend time getting to know Him through reading and studying the Bible. Knowing God also takes perseverance. Don't follow Him sporadically, but keep on following even when you don't feel like it.

We sometimes get in the habit of only "using" God in an emergency. But God is not like a spare tire that we put on when nothing else works, then take off when life returns to normal. God can't be stored in the trunk of the car, so to speak.

If we're working to know God and God is working in our lives, we will want to share Him with others, and we will gain a heart like His.

As condemned murderer Charles Peace was led to the gallows in Leeds, England, in 1879, a priest followed, calmly reading aloud the "Consolations of Religion," which warned Peace of the torment to come after death. His executioners offered a final request, and Peace asked to speak with the priest.

"Sir," he said, "if I believe what you and the church of God say that you believe about hell, even if England were covered with broken glass from coast to coast, I would walk over it on hands and knees and think it worthwhile living just to save one soul from an eternal place like that."

We have to ask ourselves, "Do we have that sense of urgency?"

God has given us an urgent task—to proclaim the Good News of Jesus Christ to the spiritually lost. But as we begin to build bridges to those we know who need Christ, we may encounter some extremely wide chasms.

3

Great Chasms
That Need to Be Crossed

CHUCK COLSON, CHRISTIAN AUTHOR AND FOUNDER OF PRISON Fellowship, was invited to dinner by a well-known media figure whom he called "Tom."

"Come talk to me about God," Tom said. At the outset of dinner, Tom told Colson he didn't believe in God. "But I'd like to hear what you have to say."

Colson began with his personal testimony of how he had come to know Christ during the dark days of the Watergate scandal, but his friend cut him off. "I know your story," Tom said and told Colson of a friend who had found peace in New-Age spirituality. "Crystals, channeling—it worked for her, just like your Jesus."

Colson tried to explain that Jesus is a historical person who really lived and died, but Tom countered that the guru his friend followed was a real person too.

Tom had suffered health problems. Maybe he had wondered about death and what comes after, Colson suggested. "Heaven is a myth invented in primitive times," Tom interrupted. "Today we know humans are just another species of animal. When they die, that's the end."

Colson tried to use Scripture. "I've studied the Bible," Tom said. "It's a wonderful collection of ancient fables." So Colson tried a different approach—the Bible's historical validity. "Some parts might be historical, but no intelligent person today can believe in miracles," was Tom's curt response.

"By now," Colson wrote, "I had been working (that's the only word for it) nearly an hour without finding a chink in Tom's armor." Tom did finally listen when Colson used secular examples to illustrate the universal feeling of guilt we carry for our actions.

Colson's struggle to bridge the chasm to his non-Christian friend is all too common. Before we discuss a few of the unavoidable chasms between Christians and non-Christians, we had better admit that we are responsible for some unnecessary ones. The Bible does say we should "not love the world or anything in the world" (1 John 2:15), but sometimes we go so far in our zealous attempts at spiritual purity that we dig the existing chasms deeper and wider, making it more difficult for us to gain a hearing for the Gospel.

For instance, a certain denomination published a yearly list of "forbidden items." If you were found possessing or doing any of the things on that list, you faced immediate rejection from the church. As you read the list for various years, be aware of your reaction as a Christian, then consider how a non-Christian might react.

> 1939—Automobiles, jazz, flesh-colored nylons, joyrides
>   to the beach or the mountains, and hanging out at
>   the gas stations on Sunday.
> 1945—Wearing your hat slanted to one side and telling
>   ghost or love stories.
> 1947—Swimming pools.
> 1949—Ruffled curtains and lace tablecloths.

1953—House plants and magazines such as *Country Gentleman*, *Life*, *Post*, and *Boys' Life*.
1957—Wedding cakes, four-part singing, and TV.
1961—Curls in your hair, wearing spiked heels, and using the term "kids."
1965—Basketball, tight dresses, bobby socks, and root beer.
1968—Cameras and flashy cars.
1969—Miniskirts, shaving your legs, wearing your hair long, and wearing loud colors.

Many of those forbidden items sound outrageously silly to us today, don't they? Put yourself in the position of a non-Christian who saw those dubious "Christian" restrictions (and even some less radical ones in various church groups), and you might understand why he would keep his distance from church folk. It's just another chasm we have to cross.

Even in our own families, the chasms between us and our parents and siblings can be enormous and intimidating.

"Jesus is the light of the world," Debbie said as her mother extolled the Eastern art of meditation. "He's the way, the truth, and the life. He's everything we need."

"But what about the millions of people who know their God by another name," her mother asked, "and who have another way to approach His throne? Who are you to say that Jesus isn't the Muslims' Mohammed or the Hindus' Brahman or China's Buddha?"

"Mom, we've been through all this before! The Bible says that the Son of God was born of a virgin in the city of David. That He will come again in a cloud of glory. That's twice, Mom, not three times, not four!"

"I *am* familiar with the Bible," her mother said slowly. "In case it hadn't occurred to you, I was reading it before you were born."

Relationships with non-Christian family members can produce some of the most formidable and intimidating chasms we face.

In addition to the chasms we have just mentioned, non-Christians have many presuppositions about God and religion based on what they see in movies, read in newspapers, and watch on television. If you asked the average person on the street about Christianity, his answers probably would reflect perceptions gleaned from the media. As unfair and untrue as those stereotypes might be, they still influence the way non-Christians live and think and feel, and they often create gaps that hinder people's consideration of a personal relationship with Jesus Christ.

What is separating you from a non-Christian friend? What are the misunderstandings that he or she has about you? What pressures is that person facing that might hinder his or her consideration of the Gospel?

Maybe you have been a Christian long enough to have forgotten what it is like to be on the other side. Let's look at a few of these chasms and remember.

The Chasm of Concern

Newsweek magazine in January 1993 carried the front-page banner "The '90s: A Survival Guide." The lead story was entitled "The Age of Anxiety," and the opening lines read, "War. Recession. Runaway deficits. Ominous warnings of racial strife and environmental collapse. It's enough to make you worried sick. But what does it all mean?"

Many people silently ask that same question. They're worried about the future of our country, our planet . . . their own lives.

It doesn't matter where you live—Los Angeles, New York City, or Anchorage, Alaska. People are busier than they want to be;

they're harassed. Their families are falling apart, their jobs are stressing them out, and they are just trying to survive.

William J. Bennett understands that our times give us plenty to worry about. In his *Wall Street Journal* article "Quantifying America's Decline," he said:

> What is shocking is just how precipitously American life has declined in the past 30 years despite the enormous governmental effort to improve it. Since 1960 the U.S. population has increased by 41%. Inflation-adjusted spending on welfare has increased by 630%, and spending on education 225%. But during that same 30-year period, there has been a 560% increase in violent crime, a 419% increase in illegitimate births, a quadrupling in divorce rates, a tripling of the percentage of children living in a single parent home, more than a 200% increase in the teenage suicide rate, and a drop of almost 80 points in the SAT rates. Clearly, many modern-day social pathologies have gotten worse. More important, they seem impervious to government's attempts to cure them.

"We've got the disease," some will say, "but who's got the cure?"

I saw a bumper sticker a while back that said, "With a life like mine, I could be on all of Oprah Winfrey's shows." I thought that was humorous at first, but then I remembered I had met a few people who actually could be on all of Oprah's shows. Those people—and many more like them—have deep concerns bearing down on their lives.

My neighbor is a wonderful guy, and he has a wonderful family. But he is trying to run his own business, and he is so busy, I hardly ever see the man anymore. Once when I did happen to see him outside I went over to talk with him because we hadn't visited in over six months. I could see the weariness in his eyes as he told me how harassed he'd been as he tried to get his store going. Probably some of the non-Christians (and Christians too) you know feel the same way. I was driving in Alaska several years ago behind a big truck with a woman at the wheel. The frame around the license plate on the back of the truck said, "I have PMS and I'm carrying a gun." I thought, *Wow, even here in Alaska they've got problems!*

Have you ever been on an airplane when the person next to you suddenly opens up and tells you his deepest, darkest secrets? I've had that experience. All of a sudden I'm hearing about divorce, adultery, and all the skeletons in the closet! Why do people do that?

A recent article I read said most people feel guilty about something and want to unload on someone, and they know they will probably never again see that person next to them on the plane! If you've ever been the one on the plane who catches an earful of someone's problems, you may never know that harassed person's name, but you'll know a good deal more about his problems than probably anyone else in his life.

The weight of life itself can be unbearable at times, and that burden can eventually drive a person to Christ. Not long ago I was preaching on the coast of Oregon in a high school football stadium. After giving the invitation to come forward and receive Christ, I noticed one man in particular. He literally dropped to his knees in front of the platform and sobbed before the Lord, "Forgive me! Forgive me!"

I later found out he was the janitor of the high school where I was preaching, and he had been washing windows outside the school as he listened to my message over the stadium loudspeakers. The good news of forgiveness and eternal life in Jesus Christ drew him like a magnet, and when I gave the invitation he dropped what he was doing, ran across the campus to the stadium, and gave his life to Christ.

As I talked to him the next day, he told me how badly he had messed up his life, including a painful divorce. Then he repeated a classic line I have heard so many times from others who have come to Christ. "You know," he admitted, "when I gave my life to Christ last night, I felt like weights were being lifted off my shoulders. I've never felt so free before, and I've never had such peace."

Many more people like this young man are still carrying around the burdens of life, not knowing there is Someone who can forgive them for all their sins and relieve them of backbreaking labor—the Lord Jesus Christ.

Chances are, a person in your life right now faces those concerns and hassles. Maybe you can be the one who makes that liberating introduction.

I love Jesus' words, "Come to me, all you who are weary and burdened, and I will give you rest" (Matthew 11:28). People all around us are weak from carrying their heavy burdens, and they have little to look forward to except more weight and more weakness. You have the refreshing message of rest that so many concerned, worried people need to hear. If we are going to build bridges to them, we must be sensitive to the burdens they carry.

The Chasm of Confusion

A cartoon I saw pictured a mother and father giving instructions to the baby-sitter as they prepared to go out for the evening. "Here is a list of the TV programs our children are not allowed to watch," the mother said, "and here is a list of television preachers they are not allowed to watch."

It's sad but true—churches, denominations, services, and

doctrines are confusing and intimidating to many who don't know Christ.

Let's confess our sins again—we Christians are to blame for a lot of the bewildering signals our culture receives. Part of the problem is the incessant failure to make our lives as consistent as the message we preach. Whenever the two don't match, confusion reigns.

In his book *Prevailing Prayer*, D.L. Moody explained how the lifestyles of Christians can actually hinder evangelism. He said:

> Can we afford to hinder the mighty movings of God's Spirit in this hour by unconfessed and unforsaken sin? I firmly believe that the church of God will have to confess her own sins before there can be a great work of grace. There must be a deeper work among God's believing people. I sometimes think it is about time to give up preaching to the ungodly and preach to those who profess to be Christian. If we had a higher standard of life in the church of God, there would be thousands more flocking into the kingdom.

The story is told about a man who cut his finger very badly while working in his garage one Saturday morning. When he showed the wound to his wife, she said, "You have to go to the emergency room right now!" As he arrived at the emergency room he saw two doors, one labeled "Under 50" and the other "Over 50."

"That's easy—I'm under fifty," he said and opened the appropriate door.

Inside he was met by two more doors. One said "Male," the other "Female." Striding through the correct door with his bleeding finger, he saw two more doors—"Upper Body" and "Lower Body." After thinking about it, he concluded his hand was attached to his arm, which was attached to his upper body, so again he pushed open the correct door.

Amazingly, two more doors greeted him—"Internal" and "External." Slightly annoyed, he pushed open "External" and—he was expecting this—two more doors faced him: "Major" and "Minor." His sliced finger was major to him, but he calmed himself and admitted it wasn't as major as heart surgery or taking out your liver, so he opened the "Minor" door—and found himself in the parking lot!

"Well," he thought, "I guess it really is pretty minor after all." So he headed home, where his nervous wife greeted him at the door and asked, "Honey, did they help you at the hospital?"

"Oh no, they didn't help me at all," he replied. "But my, are they organized!"

In some of our churches that punch line isn't a joke—it's reality. We have plenty of schedules to keep and programs to attend, but are we really helping people like we say we want to help people? More important, are we helping those who don't know Christ understand who we are and why we do what we do, dispelling the confusion that so easily surrounds religion with all of its trappings?

Your personal example of what a Christian can and should be will do wonders in bridging the chasm of confusion. I will discuss this in more detail in Chapter 6, but for now this poem by Edgar A. Guest could well express what your non-Christian friend thinks as he observes you:

> *I'd rather see a sermon*
> *than hear one any day,*
> *I'd rather one should walk with me*
> *than merely show the way.*

The eye's a better pupil and
  more willing than the ear;
Fine counsel is confusing,
  but example's always clear;
And the best of all the preachers are the men
  who live their creeds,
For to see the good in action is what
  everybody needs.
I can soon learn how to do it
  if you'll let me see it done.
I can watch your hand in action,
  but your tongue too fast may run.
And the lectures you deliver
  may be very wise and true;
But I'd rather get my lesson
  by observing what you do.
For I may misunderstand you
  and the high advice you give,
But there's no misunderstanding
  how you act and how you live.

I also want to point out that in spite of the confusion non-Christians have about Christians, sometimes we can use those questions and misunderstandings to fuel discussions with unbelievers.

My wife has been talking with a friend in our neighborhood whose big question was, "What do the Mormons believe? How is it different from what you believe?" Because questions like that are about religion—but not about Jesus—my wife has steered that conversation to present the basics of a loving heavenly Father who sent His Son, Jesus Christ, to die for our sins. She used that chasm to build a bridge.

Maybe some people you know are confused about church,

but they use the old line, "Well, I'd like to go back to church, but the church is so full of hypocrites, I just can't go anymore."

I hear that often. I like it when people say that because I tell them, "You're right. The church is full of hypocrites, because a hypocrite is someone who is pretending to be something he isn't. That's why Jesus blasted the Pharisees, because they pretended to love God. They pretended to love people. They pretended to do good things for mankind. Jesus boldly told them, 'You have no love. You don't show mercy. You don't show justice. You do anything but that.' Jesus called the Pharisees hypocrites too, and they were the religious elite of their day.

"I can be a hypocrite, and so can you, whenever we pretend to be what we aren't. We can pretend we are committed to the Lord. We can pretend we are reading our Bible regularly. We can pretend to have a wonderful prayer life. We are all hypocrites at one time or another."

Then I share the difference between hypocrisy in religion compared with the honesty that marks a relationship with Jesus Christ.

Use the non-Christians' confusion about church and "church people" as an opportunity to build a bridge to them.

The Chasm of Carelessness

"Eat, drink, and be merry" is more than just a casual motto to some people. That's really how they live their lives.

Not long ago I heard two men talking in front of me on a plane. Both of them had had a little too much to drink, and they were getting so loud, you could hear their conversation quite clearly. One of the men started talking about an auto accident he'd been in a couple of weeks earlier. I heard him say, "You know, I can't believe it—I've never thought about my own mortality before. I've never thought about dying."

I could see this man around the other heads in front of me, and I thought to myself, *He's got to be at least fifty years old, and he's never thought about dying before?*

I started thinking about dying when I was seven years old because my mom hung that famous prayer in my room: "If I should die before I wake, I pray the Lord my soul to take." To think that it took fifty years for that man to think about his mortality!

The brilliant orator and educator Daniel Webster was once asked, "Mr. Webster, you have a colossal mind. What is the greatest thought you've ever thought?"

Without hesitating Webster replied, "The most awesome, the most shattering, the most terrifying thought I've ever had is that I am personally responsible to God, and that I will one day stand before Him."

That thought might motivate some people, but it never occurs to others. To the latter group, life is just an excuse for an extended party.

A few years ago I was responsible for the production of a TV broadcast where I did on-the-street interviews. I asked two important questions of the people I stopped: "What makes you feel guilty? And how do you get rid of that guilt?"

All day I posed those questions to women and men, young and old, executives in business suits and bikers in leather. Some of those people were amazingly careless about the guilt they couldn't escape.

A tattooed punk rocker confessed he felt guilty doing things he knew he shouldn't do. When I asked him how he got rid of that guilt, he said, "Only time removes my guilt."

An Asian American young woman admitted she felt guilty

when she treated other people badly. After my second question about getting rid of that guilt, the strangest look came over her face, and she said, "I try to push that into the back of my mind and not think about it." She got a faraway look in her eyes, then quickly glanced back at me and added, "But you know, it doesn't work. It just doesn't work."

Every person I talked to that day felt guilty about something. All of them knew they had broken God's laws, but many of them simply didn't care about that guilt. They were going to live it up, have a wonderful time, and try not to think that one day it's all going to end.

We don't like to be reminded of our mortality, do we? A few years ago a clock manufacturing firm came up with a new, innovative gift—the "death clock." Imprinted with the name of the recipient, each clock ticks off the dwindling days of the recipient's estimated life span based on actuarial tables compiled by insurance companies.

The creator of the clock thought they would make great gifts for employees—a reminder not to waste time. However, most people found them much too morbid. "We couldn't sell a single one," complained the clock's creator. I can see why.

I agree that a fixation on death is unhealthy, but ignoring our mortality is an equally unhealthy extreme. As the psalmist David prayed to God, "Teach us to number our days aright, that we may gain a heart of wisdom" (Psalm 90:12). You have to build a bridge to others that lovingly questions their careless behavior and points them to Christ. As someone once said, "We avoid the thought of death in order not to be saddened by it. It will only be sad for those who have not thought about it."

The Chasm of Comfort

Actor Alan Alda joked, "It isn't necessary to be rich and famous to be happy. It's just necessary to be rich." Sadly, many people think that's true. They've got their big house, big car, nice boat. They ask, "Why do I need the Lord?" Sometimes it's hard to cross this chasm because possessions can be so distracting.

Businessman Malcolm Forbes made a statement that has become a proverb in our materialistic culture: "He who dies with the most toys wins." I saw a teenager wearing a shirt stating the perfect rebuttal: "He who dies with the most toys still dies."

Oh, how I would like to wear that shirt when I share the Lord with people possessed by their possessions! "You've got all these wonderful things," I'd like to say, "but what happens when you die?"

One of my great-aunts was very poor as a child in Arkansas, but later in life married into great wealth. Then her rich husband died and left her all of his fortune. When she eventually was on her death bed, I thought, *She's got money, jewels, and all this stuff—but she's not taking a thing with her. It all stays right here, and the rest of the family is going to get it.*

People think they are going to pack up their bags and take all their possessions with them when they die. Somehow, they think, those things will comfort them in the next life too. But as somebody once said, "I've never seen a hearse pulling a U-Haul trailer." Neither have I, and neither has anyone else. We all know better, but that reality just doesn't register for some.

The extent to which we prop up our lives with possessions is well illustrated by Stan Schultz, a social historian at the University of Wisconsin. Schultz wrote, "We bring home the paycheck, pay the bills, and realize that we can't buy as many goodies [as we want]. Given that we've come to view the acquisition of goodies as the purpose of life, we conclude that things are terrible."

How many people do you know right now whose lives would cave in if their possessions were taken away? Those are the ones who need a bridge built to them so we can introduce them to the One who is "the life" (John 14:6).

This "chasm of comfort" is a wide one when we talk to people about Christ because the Bible talks a lot about the foolishness of placing our trust in material things. That's why it is so important that we help these comfortable people face the music and think about what happens when they die.

The Chasm of Culture

Our own Christian culture presents a deep chasm to many people. We Christians have our own language. We have our own lifestyle. We want people to come to where we are and do what we do, but they really don't understand us. Sometimes I wonder if we so overwhelm them, as we seek to give them a drink of that "living water" (John 4:10, 14), that they feel like they are drinking from a wide-open fire hose!

John Bowes, chairman of the Wham-O company that makes the Frisbee flying disks, once sent thousands of disks to an orphanage in Angola, Africa, in a charity effort. He thought the children would enjoy playing with them. Several months later when a representative from Bowes's company visited the orphanage, the nuns there thanked him for the wonderful "plates" the company had sent. The children were eating off their Frisbees, carrying water with them, and even catching fish with them. When the representative explained how the disks were meant to be used, the nuns were delighted that the children could enjoy them as toys too.

I wonder how much of our communication to non-Christians is so encoded in "Christianese" that it is often misinterpreted or totally misunderstood.

When I first came to the Lord, we went to church and sang that wonderful hymn "Redeemed by the Blood of the Lamb." *Hmmm. What's that all about?* I remember thinking. *I don't get it. I redeem a coupon . . . I've had lamb chops before, and leg of lamb for Christmas . . . But 'blood of the lamb'?*

For a person who doesn't have a church background or wasn't brought up in Christian circles, some of our words do not communicate at all. We ask folks, "Why don't you come to church with us?" So they come with us, but they don't understand what is going on in the service. We have to be very careful about this chasm.

One of my jobs as the emcee of Luis Palau crusades is to help people drop the defenses they brought with them when they walked in the door. My responsibility is to joke around, tell crazy stories, or do something that allows people to relax.

Maybe a wife has invited her husband to the campaign and he really doesn't want to go. Though he comes anyway because he wants to keep peace in the family, he sits down with his arms folded and almost dares anyone to have fun. He just knows *he's* not going to be happy. He's just waiting to see what this religious meeting is all about—and for it to be over.

A lady came to me one time and said, "Dan, I want to thank you for helping my sister relax tonight." The sister had come to the crusade, sat down in the chair, and folded her arms. Her shoulders were clear up to her ear lobes, she was so uptight. But after I started having fun with the audience, her shoulders began to droop. By the time Luis got up to preach, the lady told me, "My sister was slouched on the chair, arms unfolded, drinking a Coke and ready to listen." That previously uptight sister relaxed when her preconceived image of Christians didn't play out. And she was one of the first people who came forward that night when the invitation was given to open her heart to Jesus Christ.

Non-Christians have a mental picture of what Christians are like. When we approach them, their defenses go up to protect them from that faulty image. As we disassemble the image, we can build a bridge to them—and even have fun doing it!

The Chasm of Confidence

People say, "Hey, I'm okay. I haven't killed anybody. I pay my taxes. I don't beat my wife. I buy shoes for my kids. I give to charities. I donate blood. I am a Christian."

If you have talked to people about the Lord before, you know that this can be one of the most difficult chasms to cross. We have to get people to the point of admitting, "I'm lost. I'm a sinner. I need a Savior." This bridge is no fun to build or to cross, but it's absolutely essential if we hope to communicate the entire Gospel.

I have attended far too many funerals where I overheard comments like, "If anybody deserved to go to heaven, good old George did." Or, "Shirley should make it to heaven because she was such a good person. She always went around with a smile on her face."

Those remarks are some of the saddest in the world, and those who make them are among the most misguided. They judge personal goodness by looking at other people rather than at the holy and perfect God. Compared to Him, we all fall short, and any claim to goodness becomes an embarrassing overstatement. As one of God's prophets said in the Bible, "All of us have become like one who is unclean, and all our righteous acts are like filthy rags" (Isaiah 64:6).

People have the strangest ideas about what it takes to be a Christian. I've had people tell me they are Christians because they were born in America. As much as the Gospel is preached in America, it is amazing to me that some of our citizens actually believe they are accepted by God just because they're American.

People also are confident they are going to heaven because they attend a certain church. I ask, "Are you a Christian? Are you going to heaven? How do you know?" They say, "Well, because I've been going to such-and-such a church since Noah built the ark."

In Northern Ireland a few years ago I discovered some churchgoers thought that when you give money you're on your way to heaven—and you'll have some of the best seats when you get there.

Matthew 7:21 tells us that Jesus said, "Not every one who says to me, 'Lord, Lord,' will enter the kingdom of heaven; but only he who does the will of my Father who is in heaven."

What is God's will? "For my Father's will is that everyone who looks to the Son and believes in him shall have eternal life, and I will raise him up at the last day" (John 6:40). John the apostle repeated that same foundational truth in 1 John 3:23, "And this is his command: to believe in the name of his Son, Jesus Christ, and to love one another as he commanded us."

Even some of those who prophesied or cast out demons or performed miracles will not get into heaven, according to Jesus (Matthew 7:22-23). Instead He will say to them, "I never knew you." Getting into heaven has nothing to do with being religious or going to church, but it has everything to do with one's personal relationship with Jesus Christ. That's the message your non-Christian friends need to hear.

Whether at your work or in your neighborhood, when you talk to people about Christ you need to ask yourself, "What are the chasms here? What bridges do I need to build? What's going on in my friends' lives?"

4

Drawing Up the Building Plans Through Prayer

ACCORDING TO THE ASSOCIATED PRESS, IN SEPTEMBER 1994 Cindy Hartman of Conway, Arkansas, walked into her house to answer the phone and was confronted by a burglar who had forced his way in during her absence. He ripped the phone cord out of the wall and ordered her into the closet. Hartman dropped to her knees and asked the burglar if she could pray for him. "I want you to know that God loves you and forgives you," she said.

Amazingly, the burglar apologized for what he had done and then yelled out the door to the woman waiting for him in a pickup truck crammed with Hartman's possessions, "We've got to unload all this stuff. This is a Christian home and a Christian family, and we can't do this to them."

Hartman remained on her knees, praying, while the burglar returned the furniture he had taken from her home. He then took the bullets out of the gun he was carrying, handed the gun to Hartman, and walked out the door.

After I read the article, I thought, *O Lord, I wish I would have the presence of mind to drop to my knees and pray in a situation like that!* Then I sheepishly remembered that even in "spiritual" activities, like building a relationship with a friend so I can share Christ with him, I still sometimes forget the basics—I neglect to draw plans for the relationship through prayer.

When I was growing up in the San Francisco Bay area, my uncle worked for a steel company that built bridges. Bridges are everywhere in the Bay area. The Golden Gate Bridge. The San Francisco Bay Bridge. The Dumbarton Bridge. The San Rafael Bridge. My uncle used to work on those.

As a little kid I would listen to my uncle's incredible stories about building those bridges—the kind of stories a little kid loves to hear. But he'd always tell me, "Dan, whenever they build a bridge, there is always a plan. You don't just go out and say one day, 'Well, I think I'll build a bridge right here.'" The architects and engineers study the geology of the area, the traffic patterns, the water currents—everything. Building a bridge requires detailed analysis that leads to a plan.

It's embarrassing to admit that when we begin to build a bridge into someone's life, too often we just do it . . . without any plan. When I do that, I always fall flat on my face. I don't stop to think, *God, I need a plan to reach this person. What should my plan be?*

A Christian woman named Becky has seen many people come to Christ through her personal witness, but according to her, the key to evangelism isn't necessarily how much you know. "I've discovered that good evangelism does not always require great theological knowledge," she says. "But one thing it definitely does require is prayer. In all the opportunities I have had to speak of my faith, my strongest asset has been purposeful, daily, diligent, persevering prayer. People are not 'skins' to be caught. They are searching for answers. So I pray that they will not run from Jesus, that they will be freed of their misconceptions of Him, and most of all, that they will experience His love."

You may already pray about many different things. You may ask God's blessing on your food before every meal. You probably have prayed for other Christian brothers and sisters who have been sick or have undergone surgery. You may even pray with your kids every night before they go to bed.

But do you ever pray that someone in your neighborhood would come to Jesus as their Savior? Have you ever prayed with your kids that their friends might trust Jesus too? Have you ever prayed that the person working next to you at your job would recognize his or her sinfulness, and that you could build a bridge into that person's life that would allow you to share the good news of the Gospel?

I confess, I struggle to keep prayer a consistent part of my Christian life. I'm a highly motivated reader—I love to sit for hours and read the Bible or other books on biblical subjects. But when it comes to prayer, I flounder.

I was with a Christian businessman a while back who showed me his prayer journal, and I was so impressed. In this compact notebook he keeps the names of people for whom he is praying, opportunities when he has actually shared the Gospel with these people, and notes about how God is answering prayer as he builds bridges into their lives. He even notes when he was able to lead some of these people to Christ.

At first this man's diligence was intimidating to me, but then I was encouraged that he had his priorities straight about prayer. His example motived me to pray, "Lord, help me to be more disciplined in prayer as I reach out to others."

E.M. Bounds used to say, "It is a great thing to talk to men about God. It is greater still to talk to God about men." Let me encourage you to begin to build your bridges to non-Christians through prayer. Honestly ask yourself, "Do I really pray for those who don't know the Lord? Will I pray for the members of my family, coworkers, teachers at my kids' school, neighbors, my auto mechanic, the person who cuts my hair?" Bridges begun with prayer don't crumble; those without it do.

We could talk all day about prayer in general, but here are a few specific areas about which we should be praying.

Pray for the Messenger

"Then [Jesus] said to his disciples, 'The harvest is plentiful but the workers are few. Ask the Lord of the harvest, therefore, to send out workers into his harvest field'" (Matthew 9:37). The messenger who carries the Gospel to someone you know can be you, but it also could be some other Christian who would come into the life of the person to whom you are building a bridge.

A woman came to me one time and said, "Dan, I've been praying for years for my son to come to Christ. I prayed that the Lord would use me to bring him to faith. For years nothing ever happened. But one day in prayer the Lord inspired me with the idea, 'Why don't you pray for someone else to come into his life? Pray for another Christian messenger who will become his friend. Some colleague, some neighbor who will share the Gospel with him.'"

She continued, "I started praying that way, and several weeks later my son called and talked about a new friend that had come into his life through his work situation." The son described how he had built a new friendship with this person, and that this guy was just a bit "different."

"It was only a few weeks after that," the mother said, "that my son called back and said that he'd opened his heart to Jesus Christ—because of this new Christian friend."

That mother was not at all disappointed that someone else, and not she personally, had led her son to faith. In fact, she was thrilled! She had said as much as she could say to her son, and then God used someone else—someone she was praying for—to enter his life and lead him to the Savior.

You also might experience roadblocks as you develop relationships with non-Christians, but those non-Christian friends don't necessarily have to come to Christ *through you*, do they? Rather, our goal is that we can be part of the total process as our friends come to Christ, whether or not we are the ones present when they trust Him. We can be part of that process—no matter what happens or when it happens—if we will commit to praying for other believers to enter the lives of our non-Christian friends.

As you build bridges to others who need to know Christ, how about praying that other messengers of the Gospel will come into their lives also? Pray for Christians who have common interests with your non-Christian friends, those about whom your friends could say, "Man, I really relate to this person." Pray that your friends will listen to these other messengers and that they will respond as they hear about Jesus Christ.

Pray for Opportunities

The apostle Paul said in Colossians 4:3-4, "And pray for us, too, that God may open a door for our message, so that we may proclaim the mystery of Christ, for which I am in chains. Pray that I may proclaim it clearly, as I should."

Not only do we need to pray for opportunities to build bridges to people who need to know Christ, but we also need to pray for opportunities to speak clearly about Christ when the time is right. We need to pray for opportunities to speak with our non-Christian friends so that when the opportunity comes, we see it as an answer to our prayer and know that the Lord has prepared the way for our words.

Christian author, teacher, and theologian Norm Geisler relates how he was teaching in a Bible college, surrounded by only Christians day after day, when God began to teach him that he needed to do the work of an evangelist, even if he didn't have the "gift" of evangelism. An old hymn came to his mind, "Lead me to some soul today; O teach me, Lord, just what to say."

Geisler later wrote, "I thought to myself: Did I ever pray that prayer? Even though I'm surrounded by Christians and don't have the gift of evangelism, did I ever actually ask God to lead me to some non-Christian? That began the change in my life toward the other direction."

The next morning Geisler prayed, "Lord, I never see a non-Christian during the daily course of activities. Lead me to someone." Just as the day was ending at the college, one of the students came up to him and said, "I am really embarrassed to bring up this question. But my pastor thinks I am, this school thinks I am, I've told everybody I am, and here I am studying for the Lord's service . . . and I don't think I'm a Christian. What should I do?" Geisler had the privilege of leading that young lady to Christ that afternoon, and she later became a missionary to South America.

Geisler's confession should encourage us to pray for opportunities to talk with people about Christ. He adds:

> The most rewarding experiences I've had in my Christian life have not come from teaching, pastoring, or ministering around the world. They have come from meeting with non-

Christians and seeing one after another come to know Christ. I didn't have the gift of evangelism, but when I started doing the work of an evangelist, God started using me to bring others to Himself. When I started sharing my faith with others I discovered that people were not embarrassed to talk about Jesus—I was the embarrassed one.

Geisler's story brings up the next point. If you pray for opportunities, you will need courage as well.

Pray for Boldness

I need boldness, and you probably do too. Many times the opportunity that I have been praying for comes along, and I say, "Lord, this is a great opportunity, but I think I'll pass on this one. Maybe you could bring another opportunity along later, all right?"

The Lord brings opportunities, and we need to pray for boldness to take advantage of them when they come. Our heart may be pounding wildly, but we can pray, *Lord, this is a great opportunity. Help me speak because here I go.*

Even the great apostle Paul asked his friends to pray that he would be bold in sharing the Gospel. "Pray also for me, that whenever I open my mouth, words may be given me so that I will fearlessly make known the mystery of the gospel, for which I am an ambassador in chains. Pray that I may declare it fearlessly, as I should" (Ephesians 6:19-20).

If Paul asked for prayer so he could proclaim the Gospel "fearlessly," then I am in good company when I need some new courage. He wouldn't have asked for prayer to be fearless unless he had some fear (notice that he mentioned that request twice in those verses).

If Paul was a bit scared sometimes, it's okay for you and me to feel scared about sharing the Gospel also. Even Luis Palau, the evangelist I work with who has preached the Gospel to millions of people, once said to me, "You know, Dan, when it comes to one-on-one evangelism, going across the street to talk to my neighbor, I'm as chicken as the next person."

If Paul needed prayer for boldness, and Luis Palau needs prayer for boldness, we need it too.

It's amazing how God gives us just the words we need when we recognize the opportunity He has given us and exercise faith in obedience to Him. I remember talking with a man seated next to me on a plane, and I thought to myself, *Lord, I don't know if I can handle this.* I had started the conversation by asking him what he did for a living.

"I'm a professor at the university."

"And what do you teach?"

"I teach biology."

O Lord, here we go, I thought. *I think I'm going to pass on this opportunity.* But then I prayed, *Lord, give me boldness.* I went ahead and got into the conversation with the man, and the Lord gave me just the right words to say. It was a wonderful experience, but one I would never have had if I had not prayed for boldness.

A young soldier was once brought to Alexander the Great because he had been accused of cowardice on the battlefield. Alexander despised this particular weakness in his soldiers, and with good reason. Soldiers can't be cowards! Even worse, the cowardly soldier's name was also Alexander! "Young man," Alexander the Great reportedly said, "either change your name or change your actions!"

That story has a sobering challenge for us. We are "Christians," literally "little Christs." As long as we are called by His holy name, we are obligated and privileged to serve our Lord who redeemed us and adopted us into His royal family (Romans 8:15-17). When we pray in faith for boldness, God will answer, and the Holy Spirit will give us everything we need to carry out our task of building bridges to others who need Christ. We only need to step out in boldness and trust Him when we know He has prepared the way for us.

Pray Against Spiritual Powers

Again quoting Paul, "And even if our gospel is veiled, it is veiled to those who are perishing. The god of this age has blinded the minds of unbelievers, so that they cannot see the light of the gospel of the glory of Christ, who is the image of God" (2 Corinthians 4:3-4).

Have you ever talked to a non-Christian about Christ and he was tracking with you very well, but then all of a sudden the connection between you disappeared? It feels as if you've hit a wall in your conversation, and you ask yourself, *Why doesn't he get it? I've made it so plain. What's the deal?* It could be spiritual warfare, for you can be assured that Satan does not want your non-Christian friend to hear or respond to the message you are presenting.

Non-Christians are walking in darkness, they are spiritually blind; and Satan is to blame for some of that. Even we Christians may be blind to a certain extent because we can't physically see the battle raging around us at all times. Be absolutely certain about this: Satan will do everything in his power to shut out any spiritual light you may be shining into a friendship with someone who doesn't know the Lord. This is war, and Paul says we must attack through prayer.

One thing I've learned about America as I have traveled around the world is, everything we do in America is done in excess. Even in the area of spiritual warfare, there is a tendency to go overboard. Book after book has been written about spiritual warfare; we hear numerous Christian teachers on the radio teach about the battle; we sit in church and listen to sermons about putting on the armor of God so we can defeat the Devil. I fear that we've heard so much about spiritual warfare that we've grown callous to its reality.

But whether we see it or not, whether we perceive it or not, a battle for souls really is going on. A spiritual battle *is* raging around us, and the eternal destinies of real people are at stake.

In my lifetime I have literally been physically attacked three times when I knew that it was definitely the enemy, and it was a very frightening experience. So although we may dismiss talk about spiritual warfare as "excessive," we can also err the other way and ignore Satan and his demonic colleagues to a fault—and to the peril of our non-Christian friends.

Satan is no one to toy with. Daniel had been praying to God for three weeks before a heavenly messenger arrived to personally deliver God's answer to him (Daniel 10:1-11). First the angel assured him, "Do not be afraid, Daniel. Since the first day that you set your mind to gain understanding and to humble yourself before your God, your words were heard, and I have come in response to them" (verse 12).

What an encouragement it is to know that God really does hear and answer our prayers! But the angel continued with a startling footnote to explain the three-week delay: "But the prince of the Persian kingdom resisted me twenty-one days. Then Michael, one of the chief princes, came to help me, because I was detained there with the king of Persia" (verse 13). Michael is an angelic warrior (see Jude 9; Revelation 12:7) who was summoned into this spiritual battle, which leads many to believe that this angelic messenger encountered demonic opposition on the way to Daniel!

Remember the Jewish exorcists who tried to use the name of

Jesus to cast out demons (Acts 19:13-16)? The exorcists said to a demon-possessed man, "In the name of Jesus whom Paul preaches, I command you to come out" (verse 13). But the possessed man answered, "Jesus I know, and I know about Paul, but who are you?" (verse 15). Then the man jumped the shocked exorcists and beat them silly, so that "they ran out of the house naked and bleeding" (verse 16).

In light of those incidents, isn't it amazing that Christians can hobble Satan and his legions when they go to God in prayer in the name of the Lord Jesus Christ! "Our struggle is not against flesh and blood," Paul reminds us, "but against the rulers, against the authorities, against the powers of this dark world and against the spiritual forces in the heavenly realms" (Ephesians 6:12).

Is it any wonder that a few verses later the apostle asks for prayer and petition—"And pray in the Spirit on all occasions with all kinds of prayers and requests. With this in mind, be alert and always keep on praying for all the saints. Pray also for me, that whenever I open my mouth, words may be given me so that I will fearlessly make known the mystery of the gospel" (verses 18-19)?

I have been part of Luis Palau campaigns around the world for over ten years, and one of the benefits I enjoy is sitting on the platform, watching the people come during the invitation to trust Christ as their Savior. Whether it's in the United States, Asia, Europe, or South America, sometimes you can sense a war going on. All of a sudden there's confusion, and things are breaking. Sound equipment is going crazy, even though it has worked perfectly all week. People are running. Weird things are happening.

I've sat there on the platform praying, *Lord, bring victory. Overrule. Stifle the enemy's attacks.* As I am praying, all of a sudden I feel an incredible peace—a hush. Everything is calm and quiet, the sound equipment is working, the people have settled down. I think, *Wow, that must have been an ugly battle, but the Lord won.* Then the invitation is given, I see a flood of people come forward to receive Christ, and I realize once again that this is spiritual warfare. This is an intense battle for eternal souls. Satan won't let go of his slaves without a fight.

I sometimes find myself coming to campaign meetings somewhat flippant. I think, *This isn't the right attitude—this is war!* We must be careful to never underestimate Satan. We must put on the armor of God (Ephesians 6:11-18). As you are praying for friends and trying to build bridges into people's lives, realize that the enemy is not going to stand by idle. He'll throw all kinds of distractions in your way, because too much is at stake.

Pray for People You Know Who Need to Know Christ

William Booth, founder of the Salvation Army, saw a vision— whether it was a dream or an illustration he heard or a picture he saw in his mind or whatever—that was instrumental in motivating him to reach thousands of people for Christ during his lifetime.

He saw a stormy ocean filled with thousands of hopeless people screaming for help and struggling for safety. Dark clouds hovered overhead, and lightning flashed menacingly. In the midst of the ocean was a huge rock, a virtual mountain, that rose out of the waters and stretched into the clouds. Around the rock—above the waves—stretched a platform filled with people. A few of those on the platform were lowering ropes and ladders to the people perishing in the waters below. Some of the platform people even cast boats into the waters to rescue whomever they could. But the compassionate rescuers were few. Most of the platform people went on with their lives oblivious to those in the ocean—even their drowning friends. The platform people heard the cries, but they spent most of their time tending their gardens, raising their families, and begging God to one day bring them safely to the top of the mountain. After a vision like that, William Booth was compelled to take Christ to his world. He refused to allow apathy or distraction keep him from reaching the lost for his Savior.

Look at the world around you. The houses in your neighborhood that hold hurting, hopeless people. The people at your work who are looking for someone or something to turn to, but haven't a clue who or what that person or thing might be. Look at the seas around your platform. Chances are, you've heard the cries for help. Are you reaching out to the perishing?

Let's get very practical now. Who are the people to whom you need to build a bridge? Maybe this is the first time you have seriously thought about this. Maybe you are like I was years ago when my whole world was within the four walls of the church, and Jesus told me to get outside those walls and go where the people are. Whatever your situation is, take a moment right now to jot down the names of five people in your life who need to know the Lord, five people who need a bridge built to them so they can receive the good news of the Gospel message.

You might be saying, "Dan, I don't have any non-Christian friends." Consider the various spheres of influence you have. That might include people you haven't thought about before. Survey your work relationships, your business relationships, your social relationships. In an attitude of prayer, write down those names right now. And if you truly don't know anyone who needs to know Christ, pray, "Lord, give me a person to whom I can build a bridge."

Don't be too quick to delete someone from your mental list of non-Christian friends to pray for. Author Rebecca Manley Pippert reminds us that *anyone* without Christ desperately needs Him. "Have you ever met a person and instantly concluded, *Oh, he'd never be interested in the gospel,* only to discover how wrong you were?" Pippert asks ("Gaining the Right to Be Heard, *Moody,* November 1985, p. 27). "If so, you are in good company. The disciples crossed the Samaritan woman off their list because a mere glance betrayed her immoral lifestyle and her race. But Christ shows us we must never look at a person superficially. Instead, we should ask ourselves: *Why are they doing what they do? Are they looking for the right thing, but in all the wrong places?*" I encourage you to keep all your possibilities on the table as you consider the people within your personal spheres of influence.

I urge you to take the names you wrote down and transfer them to a card you can keep close by you during the week. Keep the card as a reminder to pray for those people. Tape it on a mirror. Put it on the visor in your car. Put it in your Bible. Put it wherever you will see it often, so you can pray for those people frequently.

A young mother named Vicki decided her children deserved a mother who would take them to church. Vicki's husband was totally uninterested in attending with the family, so Vicki began to go by herself with her six-year-old daughter Stephani and her three-year-old son Jeff. She hoped her example with the children might melt her husband's resolve.

But weeks turned into months, and still her husband only mumbled, "You go ahead" from behind his Sunday morning paper when she invited him to come along.

From the beginning her children had asked her about Daddy's refusal to go with them on Sunday. She encouraged them to pray for Daddy, always reminding them that they would receive whatever they asked for in Jesus' name. Her faith in God's ability to soften her husband's heart began to wane. Her children, however, never gave up inviting Daddy to church, believing Jesus would answer their prayers sooner or later.

Father's Day came, and the preacher announced during the church service that he had a special ballpoint pen for each father attending that day. Jeff and another little boy were selected to pass out the pens, but after he had raced down the aisle to the front, Jeff said through quivering lips, "I can't give out the pens. My father isn't here. You need someone who has a father here." He ran back to his seat and buried his head and his broken heart in Vicki's lap.

Vicki took one of the pens, gave it to Jeff, and told him to give it to Daddy when they got home. Jeff could hardly wait for the car to pull up in the driveway in front of their house before he launched out of the car door, ran inside the house, and found his father. "Look, Daddy, I got this pen for you at church today, and it says 'Jesus loves you' on it. I was afraid you wouldn't know that, because we learned it in church and you weren't there. So you can keep the pen to remind you, okay?"

The next Sunday, instead of the traditional invitation aimed at Dad, little Jeff said, "We are going to church now. You can stay home and read your pen."

About fifteen minutes into the service, the back door of the little country church opened, and Jeff smiled as he turned to look. Nervously walking down the aisle in search of his family was Daddy. God used a little boy's faith and a simple gift to dissolve the resolve of a stubborn heart.

Several years ago at the last night of an evangelistic campaign in Spokane, Washington, a man came up to me and said, "I need to talk to you. There is something I want to confess." We stepped aside to a quiet spot, and he began, "Several months ago you came to our church and talked to us about praying for people who don't know the Lord. You encouraged us to write down the names of people we could pray for. I thought this was some kind of gimmick. So I wrote down the names of five of the toughest businessmen in the city. Some of them didn't go to church. In fact, some of them I really didn't know. I just kind of did it as a joke.

"I took the card home and put it on my refrigerator, but I snickered at it more than I prayed for the men on it. Then one day one of the men on my list called me. He'd had a death in the family, and he had started thinking about spiritual things. Before the crusade ever started, that man had given his heart to Jesus Christ.

"Now that the crusade is over, I've looked at my prayer card, and three of the five men I have been praying for came to Christ. I just wanted to say that I am embarrassed. I am embarrassed that I thought my God was not powerful enough to reach some of the toughest businessmen in this city."

In every campaign I've been involved with in the last ten years, people come up to me and say, "You know, two out of the five that were on my card came to Christ." Or, "All five of them came to Christ." Or, "I had ten out of ten." Those stories are incredible, and they all started with prayer.

Becky, whom I mentioned earlier in this chapter, had a friend, Steve, who confided he had a problem with alcohol. He had struggled with it since high school, never intending for it to become an addiction. He was leaving the next day to enlist in the Navy, so little was done beyond talking about the problem.

From that day, Becky began to pray for Steve. Three years later she appeared on a TV interview in the East during which she related how God had helped her overcome her own addiction to alcohol years before. Steve saw her on TV that day and left a message on her office's answering machine. He had responded to her invitation to give his life to God, and he wanted to talk to her! Now Steve serves as a rehabilitation counselor for the Navy.

Amazing, isn't it? After praying for three years, Becky saw her friend come to Christ. Now she says, "Experience has shown me that without purposeful, diligent time spent with God, we will not have the purity or the passion necessary for evangelism. Once you start praying and staying alert to the people God sends into your life, God will begin to use you. You don't have to be a full-time evangelist, or even in ministry. All you need is a willingness both to know God better and to make Him known."

William Carey, the great missionary to India, once said, "Work like everything depends on you. Pray like everything depends on God."

If there is a secret to leading people to Christ, that may be it. Pray for other Christians to enter the lives of those to whom you are building bridges. Pray for God-given opportunities to tell the Good News. Pray for boldness, so you won't let those opportunities pass by without breaking your silence and stepping out in faith as you speak of your Savior. Pray for the Holy Spirit to bust through the spiritual battle lines that surround your friend who needs to know Christ. Pray as you survey your world, your coworkers, and your neighbors, asking God to burden you for specific people to whom you could build a bridge.

Prayer is the plan that lays out the bridge that spans the chasm to your friend who desperately needs to know Christ. As S.D. Gordon once said, "Prayer is striking the winning blow. Service is gathering up the results."

5

Bridges vs.
Barriers

NOW THAT YOU'RE DRAWING UP PLANS THROUGH PRAYER TO BUILD bridges to your non-Christian friends, we need to talk about the tools you will use to begin the construction.

Studies conclude that people normally have seven to nine contacts with the Gospel message before they make a decision for Jesus Christ. That is very helpful for me because often I don't know where people are in that process when I begin to build a bridge to them. Maybe when I share the Gospel with them, that is contact number three, or maybe it's contact number nine. It may not be obvious what God is doing in their lives at that particular time or how much exposure to the Gospel they have had; so how we approach them is important.

I told you about my bridge-building uncle in the last chapter. He said you always draw up a plan before you begin to build a bridge. He also told me many times that when you build bridges, there is a correct tool for every kind of job. Some of the nuts and bolts on the Golden Gate Bridge or the San Francisco Bay Bridge are absolutely gigantic. I've always wondered what kind of a wrench the workers used to tighten them. But you can be sure that whatever tool they used, they used the tool specifically designed to tighten gigantic nuts and bolts.

When we talk to people and build bridges to them, we need the right kind of tool too. Colossians 4:5-6 says, "Be wise in the way you act toward outsiders. Make the most of every opportunity. Let your conversation be always full of grace, seasoned with salt, so that you may know how to answer everyone." An important phrase in that verse is, "Be wise." Don't use the wrong communication tool on the wrong person. Don't try to tighten nuts and bolts with a screwdriver.

As we talk about using the right tool to build a bridge to someone, let's remind ourselves that we will be using *conversational evangelism*, not *confrontational evangelism*. We're not talking about approaching someone on the street whom we've never seen and laying the Gospel on them cold turkey. Some people are good at that, and if you are one of them, keep at it! But most of us are better at conversational evangelism, using kind words that are "full of grace," "seasoned with salt" to make the Gospel attractive and tasty to others. All of us can do that . . . if we use the right tools.

Before we discuss the right tools, let's look at a few of the wrong ones, approaches we should avoid.

The Hard-Sell Approach

Think of the in-your-face car salesman when you think of the hard-sell approach. This person comes on too strong; he's overly aggressive. A car salesman wants your money, and he usually isn't too interested in you as a person. If he pretends to care about you, it's probably an act you can see through sooner or later. If you said to him, "You know, I really am not doing that well. Do you want to hear about it?" the guy would be gone!

That's how we come across to non-Christians sometimes. We act like we care, but what we really want out of the person is a decision for Christ. We might feel that pushing them into that decision is doing them a favor, but usually we aren't doing them a kindness when we act like that. Furthermore, once it becomes clear that we are interested in getting something from them, the bridge begins to crumble.

I was in an elevator in Phoenix, Arizona, when the door opened and three well-dressed women got on to go to a higher floor for lunch. One floor up, the elevator door opened again. A man got on, and as soon as the door closed, he spun around to face the three startled women and me. With glassy eyes, he launched into a lecture about how they were sinners going to hell and needed to repent and come to God. For fifteen floors we endured his tirade. Then the doors opened, he left, and suddenly it was quiet again.

One of the ladies broke the awkward silence with, "What a jerk!" Another chimed in, "What a fool!" They also used more descriptive words I won't repeat to convey their shock and embarrassment. I thought to myself, *That guy probably did more harm in thirty seconds than any possible good he might have done for the Gospel.*

That's the hard-sell approach at its worst, but we all can be guilty of it to one degree or another. This probably isn't the kind of tool you need.

A Christian man named Randy has trained people in personal evangelism for years, and he has said, "Once people have learned to share the Gospel, they often forget how to act normally when talking about Jesus. It's almost as if the training itself displaces their naturalness. Their voices take on a compulsory, demanding tone. Instead of sounding conversational, they come across as mechanical and preachy. People can sense something unnatural."

There's that word again—*conversational.* Think of it this way. Would you rather have someone preaching in your face or listening and responding thoughtfully to your words? So do the friends you will make for the sake of the Gospel.

A Christian friend, Angeline, summarized her growth in sharing her faith this way: "I used to approach people with a fixed agenda, armed with a memorized Gospel presentation. These information-dumping sessions meant little to my hearers. Now I allow them to 'evangelize' me, to educate me about what they believe and why. Once I understand them, I can respond more relevantly. And they are more ready to listen once they feel they've been heard."

Angeline makes a good contrast that we need to keep in mind: the rigid, hard-sell approach is at one end of the spectrum in evangelism, and listening and responding relevantly are at the opposite end. We'll talk more about listening in the next chapter, but for now remember that when you are sharing the Gospel with someone, the straightforward approach will probably repel more people than attract them.

The Pious Approach

The person who uses this approach is usually so heavenly-minded that he or she is no earthly good. I actually used this approach for a few years, and it didn't work very well. All my attention was focused inside the four walls of the church, and about all I read were commentaries. I was doing a lot of good things, but I didn't have a clue what the average person on the street thought about life or what he was going through. I had become too sheltered, too insulated from people.

Finally my mom said to me, "You've got to start reading some different things and being around different people," and she was right. I needed to find out what was going on in life, what people were struggling with. That's why now I like to be around laypeople and business people who have to relate to others on a daily basis.

One of the best examples I've had in this area is Luis Palau. He reads a lot and really pays attention to what is happening in the world.

Before I started working with the Palau team, I had never picked up a *Wall Street Journal*, for example. Now I read business magazines and anything else I can get my hands on. What amazes me is that once you begin to read more widely and gather information, it's a little easier to talk to people. Why? You understand what is important to them, what has captured their attention, and what they feel comfortable talking about. The more we stay away from the pious approach and instead try to understand the world of non-Christians, the easier it will be to build bridges to them.

The Social-Misfit Approach

Do you remember the Rainbow Man who used to be seen in the stadiums at televised sporting events? He wore this wild Afro-type, rainbow-colored wig and held up a gigantic sign that said "John 3:16," making sure he was likely to be on-camera at key moments of the game. I always wondered how he got such good seats at all the major sporting events. I also wondered how many people ever came to the Lord through his "ministry." My friends would see him on TV and remark, "Who's the nutcase?"

The social misfit thinks he has to be weird to attract attention for the Lord. Some wear buttons that say "Turn or burn" or "Get right or get left." Don't misunderstand me. Wearing clothing or jewelry that conveys some Christian message is not wrong. My sons wear Christian T-shirts and necklaces with crosses to school all the time. There is nothing wrong with that. But sometimes we can go so far that we become a *distraction*, not an *attraction* for Jesus.

First John 2:15-16 reminds us that we are *in* the world (this is where we live and exist), but we are not to be *of* the world (we can't let the world's values influence us). We still have to pay our taxes and make our house payments. We still have to drive a car and wear clothing. We still have to live here on Planet Earth with a few billion people who don't know Jesus. However, while we go through life we can still be normal and love God and build bridges to other people. We just have to use the right tools for the job.

Your Most Valuable Tool

The Institute of American Church Growth polled more than 14,000 Christians and asked them, "What or who was responsible for you coming to Christ?" Ninety percent of the responders stated that a friend or relative who cared for them and invested time in them was the primary factor in their decision to accept Christ as their Savior.

Ironically, most of us lose our non-Christian friends within two years of coming to Christ. How are we going to lead someone to Christ if we don't have even one non-Christian friend with whom we are spending time and developing a relationship?

Jesus spent more time with people in their homes and in the marketplace than in the religious settings of the temple or the synagogues. A classic example of this is Jesus' encounter with the Samaritan woman at the well in John 4. His conversation with her, eventually leading to her trust in Him as the Messiah, began at a common place (a well) around a common interest (a drink of water).

A while back I began to realize that many times the right tool for building bridges to people is an activity you enjoy—a hobby or a sport, for example. We always think about taking someone to church so they can hear the Gospel, but sometimes God wants to use the things we do in life to reach others, especially if they share our interest.

When Deb and I got married, I quickly discovered something about her. She was into this thing called "crafts." You glue things. You sew things. You create things. Within the first year of our marriage, our second bedroom was taken over by crafts. Honestly, I couldn't have forced my way into that room if I had wanted to.

Deb used her hobby to build bridges into the lives of women who were just as interested in crafts as she was. She does this very, very well, and she also has fun doing it.

Deb and I were at our sons' gymnastics class one time when all of a sudden I couldn't find her anywhere. Then I noticed she was talking to another woman nearby. Later in the car I asked her, "Did you know that woman you were talking to?"

"Oh no," she said, "but we discovered that we will be taking this doll painting class together." When it comes to crafts, Deb knows no strangers.

Another time Deb came home from our boys' school and said she wanted to join the Boosters Club to raise money for the school. "How do they raise money?" I asked.

"Well, they do these craft projects and then sell them at shows." *Oh great,* I thought, *more crafts in the house!*

Later on she wanted to join the Mothers in Touch program at school. "What do they do?" I asked innocently.

"They pray for the students and the teachers," she began,

"and they make crafts as gifts for all the teachers." *Here we go again,* I thought.

But you know, every time Deb has been involved in a new craft activity, God has given her someone to whom she has built a bridge for the purpose of sharing her life and the Gospel.

When we were still just visiting what is now our home church, the director of women's ministries came up to us after a service and told us about the craft classes they were creating so women could bring their friends and build relationships. My wife literally began to cry. I thought, *Praise the Lord. Somebody finally figured out that you can use a variety of ways to get people to church and still have fun.*

One year my son was playing baseball and had a coach who was a really nice guy. I thought, *I need to develop a relationship with this man,* so I tried to talk with him. Men sometimes don't make new relationships easily, and I was struggling to build a bridge into his life.

My wife went to the ballpark one evening, met the coach's wife, and in two minutes we had an invitation to dinner at the coach's house! I had been working on that for a couple of weeks! How did she do it? They began talking about crafts—a common interest.

A few years ago Deb had to be hospitalized while she underwent an operation. I took time off to be Mr. Mom and take care of our boys for five days. Things began arriving at our doorstep during the day. Food. Presents. Cards. Flowers. I'd go to the hospital and say to Deb, "We had a nice meal tonight. It was provided by So-and-So. I don't know who that is. Do you?"

"Oh yeah, that's the person I'm making a quilt with," she responded.

"I don't know this other person either. Who is that?"

"Oh, we're in a craft class together."

As I listed all the names, I realized it wasn't the people from church who were taking care of our family. It was all the people with whom Deb had developed relationships—people who didn't know the Lord.

"Who is this person?" I asked again.

"She lives in the blue house two streets behind us."

How did she know her? My wife is also the Avon lady of our community. She knows all the women in the neighborhood.

Deb's example put me to shame. What was I doing to build bridges to people? As I thought more about that, I prayed, *Lord, I've got only one vice in my life—tennis. I love to play tennis. Can I use that to build bridges to people?* I joined a local tennis club so I could meet people and develop relationships with those who needed to know the Lord—and play the game I love!

Every Tuesday night was men's doubles night at the tennis club, and I was paired with several different men in the first few weeks. Nothing seemed to click between me and any of my partners until I met Ken. After we played on the same team one Tuesday evening, he said, "I think we are pretty evenly matched. Why don't we get together sometime and knock the ball around between us?"

Ken and I began to meet regularly after that, sometimes three or four times a week, and since then we have developed a wonderful friendship. We pound each other on the court, and in that process we've gotten to know each other off the court too. Ken is a doctor, works about three days a week, then takes off the rest of the week to do what he wants. I've shared with him that I am involved in Christian communications and broadcasting, and he's been intrigued with that.

One day Ken asked me how I got involved with my work as a minister, and I shared my testimony with him. He is also intrigued with all the traveling I do, and often I will bring back a present for him from the country where I have been ministering. Ken hasn't come to Christ yet, but the bridge definitely is in place.

Do you drink coffee? Did you realize you can use a common interest in coffee to get to know other people? Deb uses a coffee-house in our area as a meeting place with her non-Christian friends.

A Christian man, Robert, took a part-time job in a men's gift shop in a local mall just so he could begin developing relationships with men outside his circle of Christian friends. The first night he met Matt, a 6'3" bearded mountain. *This is who I'm going to evangelize?* Matt wondered. *What could we possibly have in common?*

In less than an hour, Robert learned Matt had a keen interest in magic tricks and worked part-time as a professional magician.

Robert was thrilled because he had been raised by a minister father who had incorporated sleight-of-hand into his children's sermons. He soon learned Matt had read some of the same books he had read about the legendary escape artist Harry Houdini, they had both visited the same local magic shops, and they had both learned the same way to make coins disappear. God had given Robert and Matt plenty to talk about!

Karen, like me, had a passion for playing tennis and prayed, "With my ordinary life, how is it possible for me to be a light to those who don't know You?" *A tennis racket*, she thought. So she joined a neighborhood tennis team and met fifteen women the first day, most of whom did not share her faith.

She worked at keeping her language clean during the team's matches, maintaining a positive attitude under pressure, and refusing to gossip. Her honesty in close line calls was soon noticed by her teammates. She began praying for them and waiting for an opportunity to share.

Cassie called Karen one day and asked if she could play in a foursome on Sunday at 9 A.M. "No, that's the time our family has set aside for worship at our church," Karen replied.

"We need to get back to church," Cassie said. "My husband isn't interested, but I feel like the girls and I need it. Where do you go? Would it have anything for the kids?"

It turned out that Cassie didn't go with Karen to church because of a standing tennis date her husband had made for Sunday mornings. But word soon got around through Cassie that Karen was not available Sunday mornings. Seeing Karen's love for the sport, her teammates also saw the priority the Lord had in her life. One by one, others approached her to talk about spiritual things.

Pam was a very insecure member of the tennis team, and it was not unusual for her to burst into tears after a loss. "Pam, you can't worry about what everyone else thinks of you or your game," Karen told her one day. "God sees you for who you are, not for what you do." Pam absorbed Karen's words about God's acceptance and how He could free her from her constant need for approval. She wanted to believe Karen, but the truth was still hard for her to accept.

Marilyn was a Jewish teammate who shared Karen's love for tennis. She confided to Karen her disillusionment with religion. "Judaism means nothing to me," Marilyn said. "I participate in the rituals because it's part of my culture, but I have no sense of God's presence. I have no reason to believe He even exists."

When Marilyn discovered that Karen wrote for Christian publications, she probed further. "Do you believe God is really a person? What's He like? How does He communicate with you?" Karen simply told her how God had become her best friend.

"I wish I could know Him like that," Marilyn said.

With her heart pounding in her chest, Karen explained how she could.

It was obvious that Marilyn was not ready to make a decision for Christ that day, but Karen learned a valuable lesson. "It was then I realized that influencing others for Christ is a long-term project. Whatever difference I hoped to make in my friends' lives would not come through hit-and-run evangelism. It would come through my day-to-day involvement in their lives, by being in the right place at the right time." Being in the right place at the right time was possible only because she shared a common interest with the other women.

Have you ever thought about using activities such as those mentioned below as shared interests through which you can build bridges to others?

Community clubs (for example, Kiwanis, Rotary, or Lions Club). The service projects sponsored by these organizations can be a great way to meet people and develop new friendships as you work together.

PTA involvement. Most everyone in PTA is interested in their kids or they wouldn't be involved! And most PTAs are long on activities and short on volunteer help.

Coaching or sponsoring local youth sports. Baseball, football, basketball, soccer, tennis, even bowling. Call your area Y or youth league office and ask if they need help. You'll meet plenty of parents, I guarantee!

Monday Night Football. If you are glued to the TV every Monday night during football season, why not order a pizza or buy some munchies and invite the other neighborhood sports addicts over? (If you have a big TV, so much the better!)

Be creative. What do you like to do in your spare time? Chances are, plenty of others share your interests. Take the first step. Reach out to them.

Just by Being a Mom

Michelle Palau moved to a Chicago suburb with her husband, Kevin, and their boys in 1995 as Kevin helped prepare for Luis Palau's *Say Yes Chicago* campaign. Michelle's temporary stay in the Windy City could have been little more than a new apartment in a new town with new friends. But she knew God had placed her there for a reason, and she wanted something more.

"As we packed our new mittens and boots for Chicago, I recall asking God to answer two heartfelt requests," Michelle said. "First, that He would use our months in Chicago to deepen our love for Christ. Second, that He would use our family to introduce someone to Him personally.

"Trips with our two toddlers to the library, children's museum, park, and even McDonald's became prayer sessions for me. I looked into the eyes of other busy moms and asked God to guide me into new friendships that might produce eternal results. Soon I was enjoying the company of several moms my age. We shared sympathy over ear infections, tips on child-rearing, and pizza at birthday parties. Silently I'd always pray, 'Lord, how will you use *this* to reveal Yourself?'

"I frequently met Katie at a favorite cafe. She also had two sons. Much of our time was spent reminding our boys to sit down, but we enjoyed getting to know each other. Katie had gone to church as a child, but since college and the demands of a career, she had tabled any thoughts of serious commitment to God. Now, however, Katie was rethinking the benefits of church. She wanted her boys to have a solid moral foundation.

"As *Say Yes Chicago* drew near, my friends became more curious. One afternoon Katie called and asked me to meet her at the cafe. She had a baby-sitter for the afternoon, and amazingly enough, Kevin had a break in his schedule, so he could look after our boys.

"'All right, I've known why you're here in Chicago for a year now, and I've decided it's time to ask you some questions,' Katie said halfway through our meal. 'How does a thinking person develop a real faith? How does Christianity fit in with a strong marriage? How does Jesus change your everyday life?' Wow! It was exciting to share how Christ had changed my life. Several months later, I invited Katie to hear Luis speak at an evangelistic breakfast. She hugged me when I gave her a ticket.

"That morning Luis presented the Gospel with exceptional clarity. I could tell Katie was absorbing every word. At the close of the message, she marked a box on her decision card and we headed for the car. On the way home, I let Katie talk. I wanted to be sure the words were her own as she explained what God was doing in her life. She talked about the need to focus her life on God and to look to Him for the solutions she needed.

"Weeks later, as the time neared for us to leave Chicago, Katie told me with tears in her eyes, 'Before we even sat down at the breakfast, I knew clearly that Jesus had died for me and He wanted me to commit myself completely to Him!'

"I praise God for answering Katie's call to Him and for allowing me to be part of the process!"

Michelle used a common bridge that all moms share—their children. As she developed relationships through that common bond, curiosity, dialogue, and then trust were the natural results. Because Michelle was praying with a watchful eye toward sharing her faith, God blessed her desire to communicate the eternal truth of the Gospel.

I was in Chicago a few years ago when a man reminded me that we can also use painful experiences to reach others. "You know, Dan," he said, "I work with people who live on the streets. I work with gang members and drug pushers. And I was one of them once. How I used to live is how they are living now, and that's why we can relate. If you were to go down there with me now, they would probably kill you. But I've been there. I've lived under the overpasses. I've lived in a cardboard box. I've used the same language they use. I know what it's like; so when I talk with them, we are on the same level."

What past difficult experiences could you use to build bridges to people who are going through the same trials right now?

Look at the names you wrote down earlier. What would you enjoy doing with them? Sometimes we think, "If I don't share the Lord with that person right away, I'm a failure." I didn't build bridges to people at first because of the false guilt I would have if I didn't share Christ as soon as possible—and the failure I'd be if they didn't accept Him.

Then I realized that I can be friends with these people. I don't have to take on their lifestyle. I don't have to take on their language. I don't have to be contaminated by them. Jesus said, "Be a light," and to be a light you have to go where people are and spend time with them. Understanding this new approach was helpful and liberating.

In building these bridges, it is important that you take time to listen to God. When you came to the Lord—however many years ago that was—you were listening to His voice. It wasn't audible, but you knew in your heart that He was saying to you, "Come to Me."

Are you still listening to God's voice? Do you believe He will still talk to you and you can still hear Him? We have to be in touch with Him as we pursue these relationships, because His way of reaching into a person's heart is often different from ours. We may feel that our interests, our hobbies, and our experiences are insignificant and that God couldn't possibly use them. But we underestimate His ability to use these things to transform lives, and that's why we must be in touch with Him when He decides to do just that.

I love the Bible story about Elijah making an appointment to meet God face to face in front of a cave (1 Kings 19:9-14). Elijah had just defeated 850 pagan prophets in an awesome display of God's strength and power on Mt. Carmel (1 Kings 18:16-40).

In a moment of weakness, however, Elijah had fled into the Judean wilderness after a death threat from wicked Queen Jezebel (19:2-3). From there he made the long journey to Mt. Horeb, "the mountain of God." In a cave in the mountain, Elijah complained to God, "I have been very zealous for the LORD God Almighty. The Israelites have rejected your covenant, broken down your altars, and put your prophets to death with the sword. I am the only one left, and now they are trying to kill me too" (verse 10).

As Elijah emerged from the cave at the Lord's command, God sent a strong wind, an earthquake, and a raging fire. But God was in none of those. Then He sent a gentle breeze, and He was in the breeze, assuring Elijah that He had preserved 7,000 faithful Israelites who had not bowed the knee to the pagan god Baal.

God could use impressive displays of His power to get the attention of your non-Christian friends. He is completely capable of writing out John 3:16 in the clouds of the sky, for instance. But more often He seems to choose quieter, gentler methods, using people like you and me, tucked away in this community and that neighborhood. Regular people. People who haven't bowed their knee to the gods of their culture.

Sometimes He reminds us about that in a gentle whisper and

in the same way points us to people who need Him. But we have to listen to Him to hear what He's saying. We can pray for people, design a plan for bridging the chasm between us and them, and understand all the right and wrong tools to use in reaching them, but we also have to hear God.

And when He speaks, it's time to listen and obey.

6

Building the Bridge by Developing the Relationship

IF YOU HAVE BEEN FOLLOWING THE BRIDGE-BUILDING PLAN UP TO this point, you have identified several people to whom you want to build a bridge so you can share Christ with them at appropriate times. You may even have identified common interests on which to build those relationships. But with those tools in hand, where do you actually start?

The father of one of my wife's first-grade students was a police officer, and my wife suggested that I meet him one day. She knew I had set my heart on becoming a policeman when I was younger, and she thought we might have common interests.

This police officer, Al, came to school to pick up his son one day while I happened to be there also, so I struck up a conversation with him. I told Al about my former interest in police work, and we had a wonderful conversation. As he started to leave, he turned back and said to me, "Would you like to ride with me some evening?"

"Sure! I'd love to."

"How about this Friday night? I'll be by about 10 P.M."

"Let's do it," I said.

So that Friday night Al drove up to my house in his squad car, and I crawled in beside him. I'd give anything to know what the neighbors who saw me were thinking! We drove around all night as Al patrolled. I was fascinated with the police calls coming over his squawk box. He was with the canine division, so I also got to meet his dog, Demon. I even asked Al if I could hold his shotgun, but he wouldn't let me! All night I peppered him with questions.

As that first night wore on, I thought, *I need to share the Gospel with Al, but where do I begin? I could ask him, "Al, if you were to be shot tonight answering a call, do you know for sure that you would go to heaven?"* But I knew that didn't fit. Instead, I just asked questions and listened. I didn't say anything about Jesus Christ.

That night was the beginning of a great three-month relationship with Al. During those months he began to ask me about myself, why I hadn't become a policeman, and what I was doing now. He brought up questions about the very things I wanted to share with him! Those conversations led to numerous opportunities to talk about my faith and to plant many spiritual seeds in the fertile soil of Al's life. A bridge was being built.

After three months and many nights of riding with Al, I got out of his police car early one morning in front of my house and said, "Al, we've talked about a lot of things the last few months. I'd like you to read this little booklet that kind of sums up what we have been talking about. Then when we get together the next time, I'd like to discuss the booklet with you." I placed a booklet in his hand that explained the Gospel message, and Al promised me he would read it.

The next week Al picked me up at the appointed hour of the night, and as I slid into the front seat beside him, he just smiled at me.

"You know that booklet you gave me?" he said.

"Yeah, did you read it?"

"Yes, I did. I got home that morning and read it. Then I got down on my knees beside my bed and prayed that little prayer at the end of the book. I opened my heart to Jesus Christ."

I admit, I lost it right there. I reached over and hugged Al— which isn't easy to do in a crowded police car. I had tears running down my face. Demon, the dog, was going nuts in the backseat thinking I was attacking his master! In the weeks to follow, the bridge I had built to Al turned into a chance to disciple a new follower of Jesus Christ.

That experience was such a lesson to me. My relationship with Al began with a common interest—police work. I learned I had to earn the right to be heard. I learned I had to listen to Al and be sincerely involved in his life. As chicken as I am about sharing my faith, Al taught me that I can build bridges into the lives of others who need to know Christ—not by being a minister of the Gospel, but just by being who God made me. Just by being Dan Owens.

Remember, it usually takes seven to nine contacts with the Gospel before people make a decision for Christ. Relationships take time to grow, to develop depth and trust. There just isn't a shortcut through that process and no alternate routes around it. Plan to spend time if you plan to build relationships.

Now that we've noted that reminder, let's get practical.

Take Advantage of Social Events

In Matthew 9 we read that Jesus invited Matthew, a tax-gatherer, to follow Him as His disciple. Matthew immediately accompanied Jesus, and in the very next verse we see Matthew's creativity—he threw a party for all his non-Christian friends so he could introduce them to Jesus! "While Jesus was having dinner at Matthew's house, many tax collectors and 'sinners' came and ate with him and his disciples" (verse 10). Matthew used a social event to move people closer to Christ.

We may be comfortable where we are, but the people who need Christ may be someplace else altogether, and to reach them we have to venture to that place that is not altogether pleasant. We must overcome that paralyzing desire to be comfortable and go where the people are.

Let me suggest that you too can and should use social events to build bridges to people who need to know Christ.

When we first moved into our neighborhood, the folk across the street invited us to their Christmas party. I said, "I don't want to go because there are sinners over there, and they're probably drinking wine and smoking and telling dirty jokes." For the first two or three years we lived in that neighborhood, they kept inviting Deb and me to their Christmas party, but I wouldn't go.

As Christmas approached one year, I was reading and meditating on the Matthew 9 story about the party for Jesus in Matthew's home when the annual invitation came to attend the neighborhood Christmas party. I wanted to say no again, but then I thought, *Would Jesus attend the party across the street with all those non-Christians?* I had to admit that He would. So that year my wife and I went to our first neighborhood Christmas party.

The evening of the party, as Deb and I walked across the street to our neighbor's house, I begged her, "Whatever you do, don't leave my side." Inside the home I just kind of hung on to her for a while. I began to watch my wife mingle with the people. Pretty soon I found myself detaching from my wife and mingling with them myself. This wasn't the horrible drunken brawl I thought it was going to be!

Know what? We had a marvelous time! And I met my neighbors that night. I found out that the man two doors down from me likes to play tennis just as much as I do (and he's become a great partner of mine since then). I found out my neighbor loves his wife just like I love my wife, and he loves his children just like I love my children. I discovered that another neighbor wouldn't let his children watch certain movies, just like me. I found out we had a lot of things in common.

Something very important I didn't have in common with many of my neighbors is that I'm on my way to heaven and they are not. But I would never have known that if I had not swallowed my inhibitions and taken advantage of a social situation to meet them face to face.

We went to the Christmas party every year after that. Then one year I said to Deb, "Why don't we host the Christmas party this year?" When the party is at my house, I get to control the activities. So instead of just eating and chatting, we talk about traditions. I ask the others what they do every Christmas that is special. One said, "We make eggnog that'll knock you off your feet!" I said, "We have a tradition of reading the Christmas story. We open up the Bible to the Gospel of Luke and read about the birth of Jesus Christ." It's much easier to share how important Christ is to you at Christmas when everyone else is sharing in a relaxed, fun-filled atmosphere.

We also have a block party for the Fourth of July. We get together with food and fireworks, and everybody has a great time. We build bridges to our neighbors at activities like that, and we've also had opportunities to talk to them about Christ.

You can also invite your non-Christian friends over for an evening of playing games. Or invite them to a movie or a sporting event. Be creative. What social events in your locale could you use as a plank in the bridge you are building to others?

Ask Them Questions

So you're at a party with non-Christian friends. Now what? Start asking questions. Ask people about their life, their work, their hobbies. People like to talk about themselves, and if you give them an opportunity, most of them will respond. Some are more quiet than others, and it may take two or three one-word answers from them before they see that you sincerely want to know something about them. But after they are convinced you are genuine, watch out! It may be hard to slow them down!

Please avoid one habit that truly irritates me, that of one-upmanship. Your friend says he recently caught an eight-pound fish, so you launch into your story about the time you hooked a twelve-pound whopper. Of course, he's got to top you with a bigger story, and soon the whole conversation has become nothing more than a bragging contest. Or your friend might detect that you are more interested in talking about yourself than listening to him. Try this instead: decide ahead of time that you won't say anything about yourself until you have asked at least three questions about the other person.

Ask questions sincerely, and when you do, be ready to put our next point to work.

Be a Good Listener

A minister began his sermon one Sunday morning by saying, "This morning I'm going to speak on the relationship between fact and faith. It is a fact that you are sitting here in the sanctuary. It is also a fact that I am standing here speaking. But it is faith that makes me believe that you might be listening to what I have to say." When it comes time to actually share the Gospel with your non-Christian friend, we can more than just hope that our friend is listening. We can prepare for that goal by first being good listeners ourselves.

My wife taught me that correct listening takes both your eyes and your ears. I'd never realized that. You can be looking at someone with your eyes, but your ears aren't working. My wife will say to me, "You're not hearing what I'm saying," and I'll reply, "But I'm looking right at you!"

"I know, but you didn't hear a word that I said."

"Yes, I did."

"Okay—what did I just say?"

"I don't have to tell you what you just said. This isn't Sunday school. You don't have to quiz me."

You get the picture. I was listening with my eyes but not with my ears.

The opposite can be true too. We can be listening with our ears, but the person we are listening to wants our eyes also. There are times when I have the newspaper in front of me, and Deb is trying to have a conversation with me. I swear that I'm really listening, but her hand comes up over the paper, pulls it down, and our eyes meet. "Eyes, ears, I want you to listen," she says. I think we men especially need to work on being better listeners!

I was a psychology major in college, and I remember watching old movies of therapist Carl Rogers. We would watch these forty-five-minute therapy sessions, and Rogers would do nothing more than listen to the patient and then repeat back a rephrased version of what that patient just told him. "So what you are telling me," Rogers might say, "is that you really don't feel close to your husband anymore." After the session was over, the patient would walk out of the office exclaiming, "Oh, Dr. Rogers, you've helped me so much. My life is changed forever!" But all he did was simply listen to the poor woman and repeat back what she said! Watching those films reminded me that many people have a deep need for someone to listen to them.

I was sitting on an airplane next to a woman when she told me her mother had just died. I really wasn't into the conversation because I was tired and ready to go home. So I replied, "Where are you going? Going home?" She repeated, "No, I'm going to my mother's house. She just passed away." I thought to myself, *I'd better perk up and listen to what she's saying.*

I began to listen with both my eyes and my ears, and then she said something about heaven and asked, "Can you really ever know where you'll go when you die?" Of course, that was like an open door to me, and I was ready. We had a great discussion, and I shared Christ with her. She didn't become a Christian right then, but I went all the way through the Gospel with her. Maybe our time together was one of those seven to nine contacts with the Gospel. But I took advantage of the situation because I was ready to listen with both my eyes and ears when she was ready to talk.

I had been invited to bring an evangelistic message to a business luncheon some years back, and the title of my message was "Is This All There Is?" I helped the audience think through their lives from birth, through school, through college, through marriage, through children, through grandchildren, through retirement, all the way to that day when they would inevitably die. And then I asked, "Is this all there is?"

After the luncheon a man with tears in his eyes approached me and said, "Thank you for your message today. I am a Christian who is a fireman, and I brought my fire chief to hear you. He recently told me he has leukemia, and ever since then I have been praying and looking for a way to share the Gospel with him. When you asked people in the audience to pray along with you if they wanted to receive Christ, I heard my boss as he repeated the prayer. On the way out to his car just now, he turned to me and said, 'Thank you for bringing me here today. I am finally free from the guilt of my past.'"

Certainly that fire chief was more open to spiritual things because of his leukemia, but it took a caring, listening Christian employee to guide him to the Savior.

I've said this before, but if you take the time to listen to your non-Christian friends now, it will be easier for them to return the favor and listen to you when it comes time to share the Gospel with them.

Look for Opportunities to Serve

A church in Cincinnati has used the novel approach of "servant evangelism" to win many people to Christ. Through small acts of kindness toward others, the members found they had numerous opportunities to explain that they did what they did because they were Christians. They approached the manager of a local restaurant and offered to clean his toilets for free. After the shocked manager understood they were serious, he agreed, and that led to several opportunities to share the Savior. They washed cars for free. They offered free cold drinks to joggers. They even put quarters in expired parking meters, leaving a note for the car owner about what they had done and where he could call (the church office) for more information. How about that for creativity!

When someone graciously does something for you, how do you feel? It kind of blows you away, doesn't it? Others feel the same way when you take the time to serve them. Moving beyond words to deeds really develops a relationship.

How can you serve people? First, *serve them with your time.* Volunteer at a hospital. Volunteer with local youth organizations. Ask the coach of your kid's sports team if he needs help.

One year I met the coach of my son's soccer team. He was a great guy and a wonderful soccer teacher. I asked him, "Why are you teaching soccer?" (I was asking questions, see?)

"First, I love soccer," he said. "And I realize there are a lot of boys here who do not have fathers, and I just want to be a good male presence in their lives."

I thought, *Praise the Lord. This guy is busy working at a computer company, but he still looks for a way to serve by volunteering his time. I need to take a lesson from him.*

You can also *serve through your talent.* "I don't have any talents," you might say. Sure, you do! Some of you are handy at fixing things. My dad was a gifted carpenter, and when the neighbor's door fell off, he would go over there and rehang it for her. She always wanted to pay him for it, but he always said, "No, no. I don't want your money. I'm your neighbor. That's what neighbors are for." What do you think they thought of Dad when he cared for them like that? Before that family moved away, Dad had gained the right to be heard, and he had the opportunity to sit down with them and share the plan of salvation. Fixing a physical door led to opening a spiritual door.

I can't fix anything. I have a Volvo that's ten years old with 130,000 miles on it. When it breaks down, it's a tragedy. I would give anything for a merciful friend who could fix cars. If you can be a weekend mechanic, I'll bet there are others like me in your neighborhood who would love to be your friend.

Do you sew well? It seems like good sewing skills are getting more and more scarce these days. You could help someone just by hemming some clothes or a curtain. Are you an outdoorsman? Ever thought about volunteering your talent for the local Boy Scout troop? Can you cook? Not only could you prepare a dish for a neighbor or a friend, but you could offer your help or recipes when you know they are planning meals for a big event.

You can *serve others with your treasure*. I'm not necessarily talking about your money, but your possessions. For instance, I knew a dad who had a ski boat, and instead of just taking the church youth group skiing, he would round up all the local kids and take them out for a day at the lake. What a great way to build relationships with kids—and with the parents of those kids.

An employer once told everybody at his company, "I'll buy lunch for anyone who will go with me to the Luis Palau campaign tonight." The meal that he bought was not fast food either! One hundred and twenty-five employees showed up for lunch that day, and they went to the campaign that night and heard the Gospel.

My son takes guitar lessons from a Christian man around the block. I found out that this guy has a number of kids in the neighborhood who take lessons from him. One of the ways he's teaching them guitar is through playing simple Christian choruses. He is serving them and getting God's Word into their hearts at the same time.

Some of you have a gift for hospitality. *Serve others by having them in your home.* If you have been blessed with a large home, you could have sixty to seventy people at a time! The Bible says, "Practice hospitality" (Romans 12:13; compare 1 Peter 4:9; 3 John 8), and I think that applies to reaching out to non-Christians as much as to Christians.

Do you have an unused piece of furniture that the local new-

lyweds or a new neighbor could use? Do your children have out-
grown toys and clothes—still in good condition—that other children might enjoy? Do you have unused tools in your workshop or
garage that someone else might need? How about cooking a dou-
ble batch of your favorite recipe, then give half to a friend? How
many of these ideas could you use with a friend today?

So many people in our contemporary world are selfish that
someone who serves selflessly stands out; such a person is noticed
and respected. Seldom will you find a more powerful tool for the
Gospel than sincere service offered to a friend in need.

Watch How You Walk

As you ask your non-Christian friends questions and listen
intently and serve sincerely, keep in mind Paul's encouragement
in Philippians 2:14-16: "Do everything without complaining or
arguing, so that you may become blameless and pure, children of
God without fault in a crooked and depraved generation, in which
you shine like stars in the universe as you hold out the word of life."

Watch how you conduct yourself as a representative of Jesus
Christ. You can be sure others are watching you.

I was interviewing a certain woman and her husband several
years ago at an evangelistic campaign in Phoenix, Arizona. I asked
the wife, "Betty, why did you come to the campaign?"

"I have been working for the same man for twenty-three
years," she said, "and I have watched his life for twenty-three
years. Several years ago he had some sort of religious experience,
and it really changed him. He's not flirtatious, he doesn't make
innuendoes, and he treats me with respect. When he invited me
and my husband to the campaign, I thought I should do it for

advancement purposes, maybe a raise. But I also wanted to know what made him a little bit different from everybody else."

Betty came to the campaign with her husband and with her boss and his wife. At the end of the meeting Betty and her husband went forward to receive Jesus Christ as their Savior. That's the power of our life when we allow Christ to live through us. As Paul says, "I have been crucified with Christ and *I no longer live, but Christ lives in me*" (Galatians 2:20).

When I was twenty-four I worked in a factory with twenty-five or thirty other employees. On several occasions working late at night, I had the opportunity to present the Gospel to several of my coworkers.

I worked there with another Christian guy my age, Jerry, whom I had known as a teenager in my local church. On several occasions I watched as Jerry flirted with a couple of young women who worked with us. I didn't think too much about Jerry's advances until one day I heard him make a crude remark to one of them. A few weeks later I heard him do the same thing, and I thought, *That's pretty bad. He'd better watch it.*

One day one of these women whom I had been praying for was in my area. One remark led to another, and I found myself talking about the Lord with her. About that time Jerry stepped into the conversation and began talking about the Lord too. "Excuse me a minute," I said to the woman, and I took Jerry around the corner.

I pinned Jerry to the wall and said, "Listen, you dummy, I've heard the crude stuff you've said to her before. You have no testimony in this place. Your mouth is foul, and the things you say don't represent Jesus Christ. Don't come into a conversation I am having and start talking about your relationship to the Lord. As far as I am concerned, you don't have much of a relationship with Him!"

I admit it—I was furious with Jerry, maybe even more than I

should have been. But you can't live like you don't know the Lord and then expect people to listen when you tell them how much He means to you.

Once I asked my two boys, "What is there about your life that makes Jesus happy, and what is there about your life that makes Him sad?" They hardly hesitated a moment before they answered. They knew exactly what they were doing right and what they were doing wrong. Most of us are like that too. We know what needs to change in our lives. Until we make those changes, we always run the risk of pushing non-Christians farther away from us (and from our Savior) rather than attracting them to us.

One jaded observer of Christian behavior said:

> Every time a Christian from one denomination puts down another denomination or another Christian, I feel glad I'm not affiliated with people who talk the walk of unity but have no interest in walking the talk. Am I wrong to suggest that the Holy Spirit wants Christians to concentrate on all the common ground, and let God deal with the rest? Instead I see churches splitting over which translation of the Bible is to be used, or what style of music is best. Didn't Christ say that the world would know who you were by your love? Didn't He say, "However you judge, so shall you be judged"? Shouldn't Christians treat that Scripture with a great deal of seriousness?

We'd better watch our walk.

Look for Opportunities to Plant Spiritual Seeds

God uses a variety of methods for bringing people to Himself. I like to use Christian literature. In this way, you're not dumping the

Bible on them all at once. You can give the Gospel to them in a condensed form, one they can easily read and digest.

A woman told me she had come to Christ because of a booklet someone had left on her desk at work. A colleague of this woman had been concerned about her and wanted to talk with her about the Lord but was too timid to do so. So she put the Gospel booklet on the woman's desk one morning, during a particularly difficult time in that woman's life. The woman began to read the booklet and got interested because it addressed the problems she was having. She opened her heart to Christ right there.

Sometimes a book targeted at a specific need can awaken your non-Christian friend to his deeper need for Jesus Christ. A Christian doctor was scheduled to do physicals on George and Nancy, who planned to live together without a wedding. They seemed committed to each other but wanted to "try out" the relationship before they married. The doctor figured, rightly, that preaching on morality would turn them off. *Might it be possible to sow some seeds in some way?* he thought.

When he had completed their examinations, he pulled from his desk spare copies of *Letters to Karen* and *Letters to Philip* by Charlie W. Shedd, books he had given to many newlyweds. "I'm impressed with the depth of your commitment to each other," he said. "You sincerely want your love to grow. While I personally believe love can best grow within the formal commitment of marriage, I want to wish you the best in your relationship. These books were written by a Christian, but the advice in them is helpful to any couple."

Six years later a young man approached the doctor in an airport as he waited for a flight. "I want to thank you for the books you gave Nancy and me," he said. "They changed our lives." It was George!

The couple had begun reading the books the evening after they left the doctor's office, and over the next few days they discovered the link between love, religion, and true commitment.

"The following week we decided to go to church together," George said. "A few weeks later we invited Jesus Christ to be the Lord of our lives. We decided to stop living together until we could get married because we wanted Christ to be the head of our home." Along with their two children, George and Nancy were now involved in their local church and were growing in their faith.

"I humbly thanked God for the privilege of sowing seeds," the doctor wrote later, "and for the opportunity of learning the results."

My dad was concerned that his mother was not a Christian. He knew that she would not be open to anything more he might say about his faith, so instead he sat down one night and wrote a letter. He wrote out his testimony and then included a brief presentation of the Gospel. Although she never responded to that letter, I always thought that was a thoughtful way to approach someone who may not want to talk about his or her unwillingness to trust Christ.

Literature is especially helpful during holiday seasons. Last year I came home one day close to Christmas, and my wife was baking cookies. "Enjoy the smell," she said, "because these are not for you."

"What do you mean they're not for me? Am I not the man of the house? Why don't I get cookies?" I joked in mock pain.

"They're for the neighbors," she said. She makes baskets with little bows on top (craft things, you know), fills them with cookies, and includes a Gospel tract that talks about the real meaning of

Christmas. Then she takes them to the neighbors as a way of building bridges into their lives.

That Christian literature you give to others can go where you can't go, speak when you can't speak, and share the Gospel faithfully and clearly time after time when the reader is ready to pick it up and listen. If you want to be part of God's harvest of souls, don't forget this important spiritual seed.

Of course, Christian literature is not the only way to plant spiritual seeds. We need to share Christ however we can, and this is one productive way to do that.

Be Sensitive to Times of Heightened Spiritual Receptivity

A British study done several years ago found that most people who made professions of faith in Christ did so after a long conversion process, not as the result of a sudden encounter, and many also said they were converted after important milestones in their life such as the birth of a baby or the death of a loved one.

There are periods in life when people are more open to the Gospel than at any other time. When a family is standing in front of the casket of a loved one, for example, it's hard to avoid the fact that one day you will be laid out in a casket too. It's difficult to be at a graveside service without thinking, "Someday there will be a gravestone with my name on it." When people are faced with life's realities, their spiritual antenna can suddenly be very sensitive.

A nurse told me that a particular patient made a disturbing comment to her as she was discharging him from the hospital. He had been depressed for several days as he was recovering from his illness, and he concluded the checkout procedure by saying, "Now that I'm getting out of this hospital, tonight I'm going to get drunk."

"Why do you want to do that?" she asked.

"Well, nothing's going right," he grumbled.

"Listen, tonight I'm going to hear a man talk about hope at the stadium. Why don't you go with me?"

"No. I don't want to hear some stupid guy. Is he a preacher or something?"

"I think you would really enjoy him, and I think he could help you out. Besides, the meeting will be over while it's still early, and if you want to go out and get drunk afterwards, you'll still have time."

That struggling man went to the campaign that evening, heard the Gospel, and gave his life to Christ. And of course, he didn't go out and get drunk that night. The nurse had the sensitivity to know that when someone says they want to go out and get plastered, he's going through a tough time. She was listening, and she heard his cry for help.

Not long ago I went to a local emergency room because my heart was beating irregularly. They strapped me on a gurney and took an EKG to determine the problem. Soon a doctor came in and announced they were going to wheel me down the hall for some chest X-rays.

"What do you do?" he asked.

"I'm a minister," I replied.

"Great, great! I'm a born-again Christian myself." He reached into his pocket and pulled out a Gospel tract. "Do you ever use these?" he asked, showing me a copy of *Four Spiritual Laws*.

I reached into my back pocket and pulled out a copy of the Gospel booklet I like to use and said, "No, I use this one!" I can imagine we looked like two football fanatics comparing their favorite team's performance the Sunday before.

"You know," he continued in a low voice, "in this trauma room people are really open to the Gospel. I have to be careful what I say, but there are times when it is the right time and I have a wonderful opportunity to share."

Here's a guy who's listening, I thought. Sooner or later we all go through tough times, and those of us who are aware of others' needs in those times will be presented with unique opportunities to change lives for eternity.

Be More Aware of the People Around You

Jesus was not so self-absorbed or introspective that he became deaf and blind to the needs around Him. Look up and look out and you will discover how you can build bridges into people's lives.

Something recently happened to my wife and me that beautifully illustrates this point. Since I proposed to Debby in San Diego, we returned to that beautiful city for a recent anniversary and spent the night in a nice hotel. The next morning we had breakfast in the hotel's restaurant. Only one other table was occupied—by an African American man and his two sons, one a teenager and the other eight or nine years old. The younger boy kept sneezing over and over.

My wife was enduring her allergy problems that morning and had a box of tissues with her. She got the father's attention and lifted her tissue box as an offering for his son's problem. At first the father politely refused the tissues, but as the sneezing continued, Deb again reached out. Finally the older son walked over and gratefully accepted the tissues on behalf of his brother.

About ten minutes later our waiter came to the table and told us that our breakfast had been paid for by the man at the cash register. In typical male fashion, I jumped up and bolted to the register, telling this father that a box of tissues wasn't worth breakfast at the Hilton and urging him to accept the tissues as a gift, without any sense of obligation. He insisted on paying for our break-fast, however, and when I pressed him for the reason, his story broke my heart.

"My wife died suddenly yesterday," he began. "She was my best friend and a wonderful mother to my boys. We could not stand to remain in the house last night, knowing she would not be there, so we stayed at the hotel."

He later sat down at our table and related the whole beauti-ful story of their marriage and life together. We listened with tears running down our cheeks, and then I prayed for him and his fam-ily. I know God placed us there to comfort them after their terrible loss. And it all got started because my wife was aware of a need around her—a little boy sneezing.

People around us are hurting, but sometimes the hurt isn't readily evident. Instead we may initially see a less compelling need that will in turn open the door to in-depth ministry—if we are aware of that lesser need to begin with.

Break out of your shell. Look at what's going on around you.

Be Patient

A writer of children's stories was having a terrible time getting his manuscript published. He persistently trudged from one pub-lisher to another—twenty-three in all—until someone finally rec-ognized his genius. *The Cat in the Hat* by Dr. Seuss has since sold over six million copies, and many parents and children who have delighted in that story over the years should be grateful for the author's perseverance.

Remember, we are building bridges to real people, not just accumulating decisions for Christ. Building bridges is a process, not a project, and it requires God-given patience.

What if my non-Christian friend with whom I play tennis suddenly said to me, "Dan, you've told me all about the Gospel, but I'm not about to give my heart to Jesus. I don't believe any of this stuff you have been telling me over the past months and years. I don't believe in Jesus Christ, and I want you to know that right up front."

I know what I would have done years ago. I would have said, "Fine. I'll find someone else who is more interested in listening to me." I wouldn't have said it verbally, but in my mind I would have concluded that the relationship was over and just move on to someone else.

But I know now that building bridges to people is a process. Seven to nine contacts with the Gospel before a decision is made, remember? Would I stop playing tennis with him now if he said that? Absolutely not! I don't know what God is doing in his life, and I don't know when a tragedy might come to his family and he suddenly will want to talk about spiritual things. When that moment arrives, I want him to think, *Dan knows about Jesus. I want to talk to him.* What a pity it would be if he thought, *Dan used to tell me about Jesus, but I haven't seen him in five years. I know I could talk to him, if I could find him. I wonder where he is?*

Often we give ourselves only one serious shot at sharing the Gospel with someone, and if it doesn't work we say, "Well, I did my best." This relationship that we are so carefully building is worth far more than one try. We need to be very, very patient.

A pastor who took a non-Christian friend to an evangelistic business luncheon told me he had been working with this man for nine years! Now that is patience. Who knows how many times this pastor had felt like giving up during those years. But at this particular luncheon the man opened his heart and received Christ as his Savior. What would have happened if that pastor had given up after five years? Seven years? Eight years? Any of those lengths of time would have seemed long enough to most of us. By our standard, that pastor would have been justified to drop the relationship and spend his valuable time with someone more receptive. But he didn't, and his friend came to Christ after nine years. How long are you willing to wait to see your friends come to Christ?

Best Friends Are Forever

Several years ago a Christian businessman in Portland, Bruce Frydenlund, told our team members at the Palau Association about his friend Greg.

"Bruce, I'm just kind of down," Greg said. "I try to run, but I get a side ache after about two blocks."

Bruce and Greg had been friends forever, it seemed. They had been roommates for five years in Salt Lake City, during their "hedonist" days. They'd been in each other's weddings. They would visit one another in the summer and call each other several times each month. Greg had been a professional freestyle skier, always a great physical specimen. Complaining about exercise just wasn't Greg.

"Well, force yourself," Bruce encouraged. "You gotta get your exercise."

Bruce tried calling Greg every day for two weeks after their conversation, out of concern for his friend. Somebody finally answered at Greg's home on the Saturday before Thanksgiving. It was Greg's dad.

"Bruce, haven't you heard?" he said.

"Heard what?"

"Greg's in the hospital."

"What did he do, break his leg?"

"He has cancer, Bruce. He's only got weeks to live."

This can't be, Bruce thought. *He has legs as big as an oak. How can somebody like that have cancer?*

Since moving to Portland several years earlier, Bruce had committed his life to Jesus Christ and had been praying that Greg would accept the Lord also. After the devastating phone call, Bruce walked into the bathroom and looked in the mirror, pleading with the Lord to save Greg. "I want to be with him forever, Lord," he prayed.

Bruce braced himself as he called his buddy in a Salt Lake City hospital. "Greg, is there anything I can do for you?" he asked.

"Send me something to read," Greg asked.

Bruce was sure Greg didn't have a Bible, so he went to a bookstore and bought one for him. He wrote inside the cover, "This is the book that my mother read as she was dying. She went through a lot of pain, but she never seemed to suffer. Whatever she had she found in here."

Bruce tried to arrange a trip to Salt Lake City, but some of Greg's friends had chipped in to buy him and his wife, Lori, a trip to Hawaii. Bruce knew he had to reach his friend soon, so for a month he prayed unceasingly for Greg. "Business matters didn't seem that important. Nothing seemed that important. What was important was getting to Greg."

Finally, Greg and Lori returned from Hawaii, and Bruce called him again. "Greg, I have to come see you." As God worked it out, Greg got a three-day reprieve from the hospital one weekend, and Bruce jumped on a plane to Salt Lake City. On the way there he kept thinking of all the billions of souls God must be concerned about. *But please don't forget about Greg's,* he pleaded.

As Bruce walked into the room where Greg was lying, he saw a hollow skeleton, maybe eighty-five pounds. It was tough to see his best friend in such a state. But as soon as their eyes met, a big smile came over Bruce's face. He could see in Greg's eyes that his spirit was still there.

After talking for a few minutes, Bruce took Greg's hand and said, "I don't know how to say this . . . You'll think I'm off the wall, but . . . Greg, you need to accept Jesus Christ as your Savior."

"Yeah, I know," Greg responded.

"Great!"

"But I don't know how."

"Well, that's why I'm here."

Within fifteen minutes Greg had received Jesus Christ into his life. "Why didn't I see this before?" he said. They read the Bible together awhile, and then Greg fell asleep.

Lori came home from work about that time, so they talked about Greg. "He's doing a lot better now," Bruce said.

"Why?" Lori asked.

"Because he's accepted Christ as his Savior."

"How did he do that?"

As Bruce opened the Scriptures and explained the Gospel, Lori asked, "Can I do that?" Within minutes she had given her life to Christ too!

Bruce doesn't remember sleeping for the next three days. When Greg was awake, they would talk. He had a thirst for the Scriptures as strong as a newborn's thirst for milk. After reading a section of the Bible together or listening to a tape, Greg would say again, "Why didn't I see this before? It's so obvious."

Bruce was back home a few days later when Greg's dad called with the news that he had died. Would Bruce come for the funeral and be a pallbearer?

Many of Greg's friends—and Bruce's—from their past "pagan" days were at the funeral. Many of them had seen Greg in the last day or two before he died. Invariably they came up to Bruce and asked, "What did you say to Greg?"

"Why?"

"Because he was so happy."

"All I did was share Jesus Christ with him," Bruce said over and over to fifteen or twenty friends who needed to know Christ too.

"Jesus is the best gift I've ever received from God," Bruce reflected afterwards. "But to think that God would use me to influence Greg for eternity—that is an awesome gift from heaven too."

So many aspects of sharing the Gospel came together wonderfully for Bruce, and for Greg and Lori. Prayer. Using Christian literature, especially the Bible itself. Being aware of a time of heightened spiritual receptivity. Boldness. God can use you in the same way if you will step out in faith to build bridges to others who need to know Him.

David Brainerd was an early American missionary who worked from 1744-1747 among the Indians in upstate New Jersey until he died from tuberculosis. He could find no one to interpret for him as he preached to the natives along the Susquehanna River except one drunken old Indian who could hardly stand. But through this unlikely duo, hundreds of Indians came to Jesus Christ as their Savior. A drunken interpreter, a devoted saint committed to serve, and the message of life—what a combination. Our sovereign God used them, and He can use you too. Are you willing?

7

Laying Down the Road to the Other Side

HAVE YOU EVER WATCHED A BRIDGE BEING BUILT? THE BUILDERS FIRST construct the span over the river, then lay down the framework for the road underneath, and only then can they pour the pavement that will allow cars and trucks to move from one side to the other.

In previous chapters we've talked about creating a plan to reach others and focusing our attention on a few particular people who need to know Christ. We've looked at the chasms that might exist between you and those friends-to-be, the right and wrong tools to use as you begin construction, and creative ways to begin to build that relationship with them.

Now we must lay the pavement that will carry us to the other side of that relationship bridge we are building.

As I mentioned in the last chapter, we want our non-Christian friends to know we value them as people, not as projects—people with real needs. They'll quickly know if you truly care about them and are in the relationship for the long haul, or if you're just trying to put another notch in your spiritual belt. To complete the bridge and create a solid road to the lives of our friends, four attitudes must characterize our construction.

The Pavement of Love

Mother Teresa came to the United States several years ago to observe work with the poor in several cities. Afterwards at a news conference, reporters asked her, "What do you think of America?"

"There is a famine in the land," she said. "People are starving."

A puzzled reporter spoke for most of his colleagues when he said, "What do you mean people are starving?"

Mother Teresa responded, "People are not starving for food in America; they are starving for love."

I once asked a new Christian just a few months old in the Lord, "What is the biggest difference you've experienced in your life?" Without hesitation she said, "I've finally learned how to love. I never truly loved my husband before. I never knew how. I guess I only really loved myself. Now I love all sorts of people!"

Unselfish love is one of the best indications that a person has truly come to Christ. Believe me, there are plenty of people in the world who desperately need the love we can give when Jesus Christ is working in us.

Psychology Today reported that given one wish in life, most of us would wish to be loved. Few people I have known exemplify our desperate need for love and acceptance more than Bill.

Bill, fifteen years old, lived on the East Coast with his divorced father. His mother lived across the country in Washington state. One day Bill's father dropped a bombshell: "Bill, I don't want you to live with me any longer. I don't love you anymore. Here's a bus ticket—go live with your mother."

Late one Friday afternoon, Bill arrived at the bus station in Bellingham, Washington. Digging his mother's phone number out of his pocket, he called her and begged her to come get him.

"Bill," she answered, "I don't know why your dad sent you out here, but I don't have time for you either. I don't know what you are going to do, but I can't take you." She wouldn't even come to the bus station to see him.

Someone at the station took notice of a boy crouched in a corner, crying, and learned about his predicament. Unfortunately, all social service offices were closed that late in the day, and there was no place for him to spend the weekend.

Someone suggested they call a youth camp near Bellingham to see if the people there would keep Bill until other arrangements could be made. The camp director agreed to take care of Bill that weekend—the weekend I had been invited to speak at a youth rally. Bill was in the audience as I preached on the love of God that Friday night.

Without knowing anything about Bill, I said to the young people, "Your mother may have rejected you. Your father may have rejected you. Your friends may have rejected you. Everyone may have rejected you. But God will not reject you. He loves you."

When I invited teens to come forward and receive Christ, Bill ran down the aisle, dropped to his knees in front of the platform, and sobbed as if his heart would break. He finally had found Someone who loved and accepted him.

By the way, a Christian family adopted Bill, and he spent the rest of his teen years in a loving home. He has grown much in the Lord since then.

It isn't surprising that love is the first pavement we must lay to develop successful relationships, is it? Jesus was quoting the Old Testament Scriptures when He said that "Love your neighbor as yourself" was one of the two greatest commandments (Luke 10:27).

Loving people is not always easy, especially those who do not yet know Christ as their Savior. But that is where we need to remind ourselves of Christ's love for us and allow His love to move in us and through us to reach others.

You appreciate being loved, don't you? So do those to whom you show love. I think Stephen, a pastor in Colorado Springs, says it best: "When you and I sincerely care about people and try in even small ways to love them as Jesus commands us, it shows. If someone gives me a call or stops by to ask how my fishing trip went, for example, I appreciate it. I'm flattered when somebody cares enough to participate in my world. That's pretty rare these days. Conversely, I can tell when somebody really would rather do other things than spend time with me."

As Stephen implied, the greatest enemy of our love for others is the selfishness that still resides in our hearts. Only through the power of the Holy Spirit can we keep that selfishness in check so that we do not push aside our non-Christian friends in pursuit of personal pleasures.

This struggle became all too real for me when at nineteen years old I was hired by a small church to be their youth pastor. The church had about 150 people, and my youth group had only ten or so kids. No matter how small the group, it seems there is always one kid who is constantly in trouble. In my group, that kid was Wayne.

Wayne lived with his mother, who tried to make ends meet as well as raise Wayne properly. But he seemed to keep landing in juvenile hall for one offense or another.

I decided I would take Wayne under my wing, give him guidance and friendship as much as possible, and help out his mom whenever I could. I was going to give my life for Wayne.

On a fall Monday evening, some friends and I were settling in to enjoy what millions of other red-blooded American males would enjoy that night—*Monday Night Football*. I was a rabid

Dallas Cowboys fan in those days, and the match-up that night was a classic—the Cowboys against their hated rivals, the Washington Redskins.

Clutching our bowls of chips and dip, we had hunkered down in front of the TV, ready for the battle to begin, when the phone rang. It was Wayne.

"Dan, I need to talk to you."

"Great," I said. "I'll pick you up after school on Wednesday."

"Well . . . I need to talk to you right now."

Right now? I thought. "Wayne, I've got a commitment already. I'm not sure I can drop what I'm doing right now." Of course, the only thing I was doing was watching football and snarfing down a bowl of nachos!

Amid my excuses, half-truths, and lies, the Holy Spirit spoke clearly to me that night. In His own penetrating way He said, *There . . . is . . . your . . . heart.*

I couldn't brush His words aside. *There is your heart.*

Sure, I wanted to be the big, important youth minister who gets pats on the back for taking care of the kids and giving special attention to the Waynes of the world. I loved people . . . when others were watching. But now it was only me and Wayne and *Monday Night Football.* No one would see; no one would know, except me, Wayne, and God.

There is your heart. I began to weep. I could not believe my selfishness, my eagerness to toss aside an opportunity to influence a soul for eternity because of a three-hour football game.

I jumped in my car and drove across town to meet Wayne, in tears all the way, the Holy Spirit continuing to remind me, *There is your heart.* I repented and learned a lesson that night that has influenced the rest of my life.

Have you ever read "The Toddler's Creed"? Those of you who have had toddlers (or still do) will especially enjoy this:

- If I want it, it's mine.
- If I give it to you and change my mind later, it's mine.
- If I can take it away from you, it's mine.
- If I had it a little while ago, it's mine.
- If we are building something together,
    all the pieces are mine.
- If it looks like mine, it is mine.

Selfishness is ugly in children. It's even more ugly in adults. I know because I've experienced it firsthand. "It's my life, Lord. It's my schedule. It's my money. It's my decision. It's mine."

Only as I allow the Holy Spirit to unclench my selfish grip on life can I be used by Him to love others selflessly and build a bridge to them.

Listen to the Word of God as it describes the ultimate act of love and selflessness:

> *Do nothing out of selfish ambition or vain conceit, but in humility consider others better than yourselves. Each of you should look not only to your own interests, but also to the interests of others. Your attitude should be the same as that of Christ Jesus: Who, being in very nature God, did not consider equality with God something to be grasped, but made himself nothing, taking the very nature of a servant, being made in human likeness. And being found in appearance as a man, he humbled himself and became obedient to death— even death on a cross!*
>
> *—Philippians 2:3-8*

Along with taming your selfishness, you'll probably have to deal with the urge to bypass people you find "weird" or "different." In my experience, more complete information about them is generally the solution. First impressions are notoriously off-target.

My wife and I used to joke about a man who was always working in his yard. He was kind of like my dad, always puttering around to find something to do. Then one day we found out he was a recovering alcoholic, and yard work was his way of keeping busy and away from the temptation to drink.

A friend, Jeff, owns ice cream parlors in the Quad Cities of Iowa and Illinois. Julie, one of the many high-school students Jeff employs, often seemed despondent. "I would often kid Julie about going through life with a frown," Jeff says.

Julie lived next to a golf course and started bringing golf balls found on her parents' property to work to give to Jeff. The deliveries were usually accompanied by a time of conversation, sometimes as long as two hours.

"I'd ask, 'What's going on in your life?'" Jeff says, "and then listen as Julie recounted her many disappointments. I began to feel sorry for this seventeen-year-old who seemed to have crammed twice as many years into her life. But all this time I had never discussed anything spiritual with her, even though I could feel that God had put a burden on my heart for Julie's salvation."

Jeff faithfully prayed for Julie. Late one afternoon as he was about to head home, Julie showed up with some more golf balls. "Should she just leave them here for you?" his secretary asked.

The Holy Spirit tapped Jeff on the shoulder. *Lord, it's after 5. I'll talk to her when I have more time*, Jeff bargained. But he felt another nudge.

Julie gave Jeff the bag of golf balls—by now he could have opened a driving range—and sat down to pour out more pain. But this time Jeff told Julie his own story of shame and guilt before he met Jesus Christ and asked her if she'd like to experience the same complete forgiveness. Julie gladly prayed with Jeff, inviting Jesus to come into her heart. Jeff cared enough to befriend the girl with the eternal frown and share with her the gift of eternal life.

It's also too easy to prejudge people with rough edges, people who seem not to need or want our love—and don't deserve it either. Who knows what abuse or traumatic loss lies at the root of a person's rude or crude behavior?

I'm simply saying this: Be patient; love people, warts and all. You may find out there is a good reason for the warts.

Nick supervised Tom at work. Tom never seemed to run out of stories about his great sporting and mechanical abilities. Pity the poor person whom Tom cornered in one of his fits of bragging. Nick patiently endured Tom's boasting and began to include him in a few of his fishing trips, as well as having lunch with him occasionally at work.

As the weeks passed, Nick discovered that inside Tom was a lonely little boy who was starving for acceptance. Tom had left home when he was fifteen and had been on his own ever since. He told Nick he didn't care if he ever saw his parents again.

Until Tom moved away, Nick and his wife had opportunities to plant spiritual seeds—which someday may bear fruit—because he had the patience and compassion to look past Tom's prickly personality.

Here is another example. Everyone knew Charles Colson's ruthless reputation. President Richard Nixon's hatchet man would walk over his grandmother to get Nixon reelected. After Colson was convicted of Watergate-related crimes and sentenced to prison, he turned his life over to Jesus Christ.

When word about Colson's "religious conversion" first got out, people were naturally skeptical. But newsman Eric Sevareid commented, "Mr. Colson has made page one with the news of his conversion to religion. The new Colson does not claim the capacity to walk on water, but he has given up walking on grandmothers."

As obnoxious as Chuck Colson was, he indeed had changed. Jesus can handle our rough edges. We can't expect the fruit of the Holy Spirit (Galatians 5:22-23) from friends and neighbors who don't even know Christ yet. Because we do know Him as Savior, however, and because the Holy Spirit resides in us, we can demonstrate those virtues—especially love—when we face a non-Christian's provocations.

"Sharing our faith is the supreme way to demonstrate our love for others," pastor/evangelist John Guest says. "We already know how much Jesus was motivated by love for people. That same love must motivate us to tell others about Jesus. Without Jesus, those people are going to live out their lives not knowing who they are, what they're here for, or where they're going. The ultimate act of love is to introduce them to the Savior. The fact that they don't ask us about Him shouldn't stop us from telling them" ("Share Your Faith Comfortably—Brushing Up on the Basics," *The Christian Reader*, March-April 1987, p. 33).

A lawyer asked Jesus, "Teacher, what must I do to inherit eternal life?" (Luke 10:25). Jesus said, in short, "Keep the commandments," which included "Love your neighbor as yourself" (verse 27). "But he wanted to justify himself," the Bible says, so the lawyer said to Jesus, "And who is my neighbor?" (verse 29).

At that point Jesus told the story of the Good Samaritan. Then He turned the tables on the self-righteous lawyer. He didn't use the story to illustrate who our neighbor is, as the lawyer expected. Instead, Jesus used the story to show that the lawyer needed to be more concerned about whether or not he was the compassionate neighbor God wanted him to be. Instead of justifying the way the lawyer excluded people from his concern, Jesus challenged him to start being a neighbor in the true sense of the word.

Stephen, the pastor I mentioned earlier, has suggested fourteen simple ways we can love our neighbors. In light of the practical suggestions for building bridges in the last couple of chapters, here are some more ideas:

Exchange simple greetings. There is a lack of general friendliness and courtesy these days.

Pass along a compliment. King Solomon said, "How good is a timely word!" (Proverbs 15:23). Never let a good deed go unnoticed and unappreciated. But be sincere.

Welcome new neighbors warmly. Why not greet them with a plate of freshly baked cookies? They will remember your kindness for years to come.

Share a meal. That's being hospitable. Often you will be invited for a meal in return, giving you a chance to learn more about your new friends.

Share a book. Christian books, yes, but also recipe books for the cook, plumbing or carpentry books for the do-it-yourself repairman, and even your best mystery book for the novel lover.

Share a skill. When you give your precious time to people, that touches them. What are you good at? Share it!

Share your recreation. Invite your friends to tag along on your outings. Do you like to visit antique stores? Enjoy attending local concerts? Look forward to hiking or mountain biking or roller blading? Maybe your neighbor does too.

Volunteer advice. You don't want to come across like a know-it-all, of course, but if you have legitimate expertise in an area where friends need help, your tactful advice may be much appreciated.

Meet obvious needs. If you see your neighbor circling his house, for example, and you deduce he has locked himself out, volunteer to help—or call a locksmith.

Watch for special opportunities. If your neighbor comes to you with a request or problem, go out of your way to help. Maybe she had second thoughts about approaching you in the first place, so reassure her that you are more than happy to oblige. People in need will not soon forget their benefactor.

Ask for help. You like feeling needed, and so do your friends. If you know that you are way over your head on a project—like changing the brake pads on your car or installing a new hot water heater—maybe a neighbor would help. Sometimes it is better to receive than to give!

Organize neighborhood activities. Block parties. Progressive meals through several neighborhood homes. Community garage sales. Baby showers. House-warming parties. You get the picture.

Form a neighborhood play group. When you take your children to a local park to play, invite their friends and their friends' parents to go along. As the kids play, you can chat and get to know your new friends.

Become active in a community group or cause. This is one of the best ways to discover common interests, and you'll be doing your community a favor as well.

Don't sit at home analyzing who is worthy of your friendship. Are you being a neighbor to those in your life? Do you really care for them? Do you genuinely love them? That's what Jesus has commanded us to do, and that must be the first pavement we lay if we intend to build solid bridges to others.

The Pavement of Transparency

Somehow we Christians have convinced ourselves that everything has to be perfect. Anything less is failure before a watching world. That's incredible pressure, isn't it? But actually as we love people, we can honestly let them know where we hurt, what we don't know, or what we're just not good at.

A pastor preaching to his congregation about temptation risked his reputation when he told them that several weeks earlier a member had given him a $100 bill after the service, telling him to include it with the morning offering. The pastor stuck the bill in his pocket and then forgot about it until he got home later that day.

Finding the bill, he absentmindedly tossed it on his dresser, intending to take it to church the next day. A day turned into several weeks, and still the bill remained on his dresser. Then he made up all kinds of excuses why he should just keep the bill and not turn it into the church. He shared all the temptations and rationalizations he faced as that $100 bill lay on his dresser.

I thought to myself as he was preaching, *Wow! That's what you call transparency!* Do you think he had everyone's attention as he confessed that he was tempted? His openness resulted in greater ministry.

If we expect people to trust us and open their lives to us, we can't pretend to be too good to be true.

If someone asked me, "Dan, do you have family devotions with your wife and kids?" I'd have to say, "Yes and no." Sometimes we are all together and can fit it in; sometimes we are all going different directions and we can't.

"Do you pray with your kids?"

"Well, yes and no." If you mean, do I have a set time every day when we sit down together and pray as a family, no. But we pray when there is a need, and we pray when there's a hurt. We pray when we are happy and we want to thank the Lord, and we pray when we are sad and need His comfort.

We talk about the Lord and His work when we drive to the mall and when we watch TV and when we sit down to eat together. God is very much a part of our family.

When we are upset or angry, we don't hide it just so others will be impressed with our spirituality. If I am upset with my wife, why not get it out and get things fixed up again rather than hiding my anger? We have to be transparent with those who see us day in and day out because when we put on masks, sooner or later they slip and the truth is obvious to everyone.

If you are building a relationship with someone and you are going through a difficult time, why hide it? I'd rather say, "I'm hurting right now, but I'm so glad I have the Lord. I know He's near me, and He always gives me just what I need to make it through."

Someone might say, "God must be your crutch." You bet He is. Sometimes I can't keep walking, and I'm glad He's there to hold me up!

We've all seen the self-made man or woman who suddenly is faced with a disaster—perhaps being diagnosed with cancer. The arrogance evaporates. We all need someone to care about us when we hit the hard times, and it is a lot easier to find people who will care if we haven't tried to live life alone.

We are all imperfect and weak, and that will become evident to all who know us—even our friends who don't know the Christ who supplies our strength to endure. Don't set yourself up for a great unveiling later on. Be real.

I am impressed by the transparency of the apostle Paul. People could see Jesus in Paul precisely because of his weaknesses and his refusal to hide them:

> *But we have this treasure [the Gospel] in jars of clay to show that this all-surpassing power is from God and not from us. We are hard pressed on every side, but not crushed; perplexed, but not in despair; persecuted, but not abandoned; struck down, but not destroyed. We always carry around in our body the death of Jesus, so that the life of Jesus may also be revealed in our body. For we who are alive are always being given over to death for Jesus' sake, so that his life may be revealed in our mortal body. So then, death is at work in us, but life is at work in you.*
>
> —*2 Corinthians 4:7-12*

If we walk with the Lord daily, people will see Jesus in the midst of our hardships, not apart from them. Then when they fall on hard times, they will listen to us because we have first listened to Him.

Max Lucado, one of my favorite authors, is adept at bringing out the humanness of Jesus' disciples. They were terrified at times; sometimes they were cowards; in between they were discouraged or depressed. They had a full range of human emotions, but we act as if we should be above all that. "I'm a Christian. I'm supposed to be godly all the time." Only God can make us godly, and He does so as we allow Him to do His work in us. But that transformation is a process, and none of us has arrived yet. We are being changed, but en route to our destination the people around us will appreciate us so much more and listen to our message more intently if we will be honest with them.

The Pavement of Sincerity

I like what the apostle Paul said when he was defending his motives to the Christians in Corinth: "Unlike so many, we do not peddle the word of God for profit. On the contrary, in Christ we speak before God with sincerity, like men sent from God" (2 Corinthians 2:17).

Paul was saying, "Hey, I was straight with you. I've been accused of manipulating you for my own gain, but you know better than that. What you saw in me is what I am really like."

Be sincere with people. Sincerity is different from transparency. When you are transparent, you are laying aside a mask you have created for yourself. When you are sincere, you are stepping out of the mold others have pressed you into. You are being yourself and not what others think you should be.

God didn't make us all alike. We don't think the same, act the same, or feel the same. We are individuals, and that is okay. That is the way God intended it to be.

When my wife graduated from a Christian college, a wife's submission to her husband was a hot topic. Some taught that when the husband said, "Jump!" the wife should respond, "How high?"

Deb went along with that for a few years after we were married. Then my dear, meek, mild, and quiet wife started spending too much time with my mother. Mom thinks women should express their opinions. She was married when she was fifteen, had her children when she was seventeen, nineteen, and twenty-one, and has been married to the same man all those years. She has also been a preschool director for twenty years. So she has a lot of wisdom about life and people. Deb would try to live up to my expectations for her, and Mom would say, "Don't let Dan do that to you!"

Over the years Mom has trained Deb to be herself, and she has learned that she doesn't always have to live up to my expectations—or the expectations of others. It has been a wonderfully freeing experience for her to discover the Deb that God made, rather than the Deb I was trying to make over.

If we put ourselves into the box of others' expectations, we might expect others to jump in our box too—even those we are seeking to influence for Christ.

Paul says, "It is for freedom that Christ has set us free. Stand firm, then, and do not let yourselves be burdened again by a yoke of slavery" (Galatians 5:1). He was warning Christians about trying to earn God's favor through returning to the Law and good works, even though they had received God's forgiveness by grace through faith in Christ in the first place.

We too subject ourselves to a kind of slavery when we think we must fit the mold others have cast for us.

A few years ago as I considered returning to work in a local church rather than continuing to be involved in Luis Palau's multi-location evangelistic ministry, one of my boys said, "Dad, you've got the best job in the world. Why would you want to do anything else?" My wife felt the same way, but for a different reason. "I don't want to live under other people's expectations again," she said.

We have to be careful not only about living up to others' expectations, but also about imposing our mold on others. We need to be ourselves and let others—including our non-Christian friends—be themselves.

There was a time when I honestly thought it was unspiritual to laugh. When I preached, I used no humor. I got up, threw fire-balls at people, said "Thus saith the Lord," and that was it.

As I got a bit older, I realized, "Wait a minute. That's not me. That's the way I perceive others think I should be."

Many times when I spoke I thought, *Man, I'd love to make this funny remark right here!* But I resisted. Finally I realized that humor is part of my personality. That's the way God made me, and I can use that to help people relax as I communicate with them.

Be what the Lord made you to be.

The Pavement of Honesty

"Speaking the truth in love, we will in all things grow up into him who is the Head, that is, Christ" (Ephesians 4:15). We expect honesty from others, especially those whom we call our friends. Is it too much for our friends—including our non-Christian friends—to expect the same honesty from us?

Someone once told me he was afraid to share Christ with anyone for fear the person would ask him a question he didn't know how to answer. We're afraid that after we have carefully built our relationship with a friend and arrived at that critical moment when we are sharing the Gospel message, that person will ask, "Yes, but where did the cavemen come from?"

What am I going to do if that happens? Fake it? No. I'm going to be honest. "I'm not sure where cavemen fit into Old Testament history."

If you don't know the answer, say so. Be honest. People will see that you don't have all the answers, but then again they probably knew that anyway. Then you can give them the answers they really need.

There are things in this life that I don't understand, and I probably won't understand them until I'm in heaven with the Lord.

I have a friend, forty-two years old, who is dying of cancer as I write this book, and his wife is going blind. I don't understand why God is allowing these tragedies, but it won't help me or my non-Christian friends to pretend that I do.

When these difficult issues pop up, I've found it helpful to turn the conversation toward Christ and the cross. Let's say a friend does ask, "Where did the cavemen come from?" Confess you don't know, then perhaps say something like, "That's a great question, though. Maybe we can talk about it later. But let's get back to what Jesus Christ did for you. . . ." A question like that, which is usually a smoke screen, seldom returns after the person has trusted the Lord.

"Don't even try to convince me I need Christ," said a dad who had lost his daughter to spinal meningitis. "When my daughter was dying, my wife said, 'God, You can let her live.' God could have let her live," the bitter father continued, "but instead He let her die."

"Do you believe that Christ really did live, die on the cross, and come back to life?" a friend asked him.

"Yes."

"If there's one aspect of God's character that is not open to question, it's that God proved His love when He took our place on the cross. I can't explain your daughter's death, but the cross has removed all doubt of how loving God is."

The father's response was striking: "Maybe that's why my wife's mother is not bitter. She understands something about God that I don't."

You need to be honest about your personal struggles too. When my dad was about to retire, he went through an unusual bout with depression. For three years he was really down, sleeping all the time, as depressed people often do.

He didn't try to hide it from those at work, though. They'd ask him, "Richard, what's going on?" He'd tell them, "I don't know. I'm struggling with this thing."

The Lord took him through his depression, and he was able to use that struggle as a way to share Christ with the men at work. He couldn't have done that if he had not been honest with his coworkers to begin with.

A longtime Christian worker, John Guest, said it so well:

"Don't feel intimidated by not having all the answers. Let me tell you a secret: People often respect you more for saying simply, 'I don't know.' It doesn't make you appear foolish; it makes you appear honest" ("Share Your Faith Comfortably," p. 33).

Lonely People Everywhere

A woman in Chicago committed suicide by jumping from her high-rise apartment. She had written, "I can't endure one more day of this loneliness. My phone never rings. I never get letters. I don't have any friends." The police knocked on the doors of her neighbors to see if anyone knew her. A woman directly across the hallway said, "I wish I would have known she was so lonely. I'm very lonesome myself."

There are people all around us who feel that no one cares—people who want to be loved. Albert Einstein once said, "It's so strange to be so universally known, yet be so lonely." Everyone—from the corporate executive to the widow in public housing—wants to know they are needed. I am too content to just walk around in my own little world. Is that you, too? We see faces on the street, on the bus, on the train. We chat a little here and there. But we never take the time to get to know those around us as they really are. And we rarely take the time to show others who we really are.

Stepping out on the pavement of love, transparency, sincerity, and honesty, we can reach out to others who yearn for someone—anyone—to build a bridge into their lives. And that bridge can lead them to Christ.

8

Proceeding Across the Bridge

AS I MENTIONED EARLIER, I REMEMBER THE SAN FERNANDO VALLEY earthquake of January 17, 1994 all too well. I was staying in a hotel in Los Angeles when I was rudely awakened at 4:32 A.M. Since the hotel was at the epicenter of the quake, my whole room exploded.

I passed my television in the air. Glass was flying. I thought for sure I was going to die. Somehow I got out of the hotel, through the fires, and back home again, praising God!

Not long after that I was playing tennis with a non-Christian friend, and we were talking about my recent earthquake adventure. I told him how close I had come to dying, and he said, "Man, it must have been frightening to be that close to death." I wasn't listening very well that day, so I just kept talking. Again he said, "I've never been that close to dying." Again his remark went right over my head. He mentioned a third time, "Man, to be that close to death . . ." Finally a little voice inside me said, "Dan, listen to the man! Do you hear what he is saying?" *Oh yeah*, I thought, *death! He's a doctor, and he has everything, but this is the one area he's not sure about!*

Within seconds I was able to turn the conversation toward

spiritual things. "Yeah, it was frightening," I said, "but you know, I wasn't afraid of what was on the other side. I was afraid I might not get to say good-bye to my wife and children, and I was afraid of getting injured and being in pain (because I hate pain), but I wasn't afraid of what would happen to me after death." That led to a perfect opportunity to share the Gospel.

I thought to myself afterwards, *Wow, we have to listen when people talk. We have to be aware of opportunities that the Holy Spirit gives us to pick up on topics that others bring up in conversation so we can use them for the sake of the Gospel.*

Turning a conversation to spiritual matters is a real struggle for most of us. Evangelist Larry Moyer said a fellow Christian told him, "I would have absolutely no trouble talking to people about spiritual things if *they* would bring up the subject. But that's never happened."

We don't have to wait for the other person to toss out a spiritually loaded topic. But how can we turn a conversation toward spiritual matters? Let me suggest seven questions you can ask your non-Christian friend that might open the door to sharing the Gospel.

1. "Do you ever think about spiritual things?"
2. "Where do you think you are in your spiritual journey?"
3. "What would you say to God if you died tonight and He asked you, 'Why should I let you into My heaven?'"
4. "I, too, have made mistakes, but becoming a Christian has helped me."
5. "How would you describe who you are in relation to God?"
6. "Would you like to know the difference between religion and Christianity?"
7. "I know you are going through a difficult time. Would you mind if I prayed for you?"

Though these are "canned" questions, they are helpful if used properly. I strongly encourage you to listen carefully to your friend, listen carefully to what the Lord is teaching you about your friend, and modify one or more of these questions to meet your particular situation.

Sonja is a vice president of a Seattle-based company and has led hundreds of people to the Lord by using lifestyle evangelism. She reads a lot and keeps up with the times, and as her coworkers bring up moral issues or personal problems, she chimes in at the right time with pertinent words of witness. "You know, our pastor was just talking about that this Sunday, and he said . . ."

Sonja has tried to develop a reputation at work of being someone who listens to people when they share their problems. Her kindness is well-known throughout the company, and when staff members talk to her about their trials, conversations often turn into discussions about faith.

Another Christian businessman shared this tip: "When I see a person reading something on the economy, I ask, 'Things like that make you wonder what's in store for the future, don't they?' I've found many opportunities to use that question to begin a discussion about spiritual things."

Someone else has suggested, "I discuss my background with people and bring up church. Even if church has been a bad experience for them, it gives me a chance to explain that Christianity centers around a person, Jesus Christ, not on attending a church."

Keep alert to national news events that people are talking about to provide a natural bridge to spiritual discussions. Legendary rock guitarist Eric Clapton's gentle ballad "Tears in Heaven" was named Record of the Year and Song of the Year at the 1993 Grammy Awards. His haunting song was played for months on radio stations around the country. The lyrics conveyed genuine grief and guilt, for he wrote the song in memory of his four-year-old son who died in an accidental fall from an open window in Clapton's fifty-third-story New York City apartment. On the night of the Grammy Awards, Eric sang his tribute to his dead son, and millions listened via TV.

> *Would you know my name,*
>   *If I saw you in heaven?*
> *Would it be the same,*
>   *If I saw you in heaven?*
> *I must be strong,*
>   *And carry on.*
> *'Cause I know I don't belong,*
>   *Here in heaven.*
>
> *Time can bring you down.*
>   *Time can bend your knees.*
> *Time can break your heart,*
>   *Have you beggin' please.*
> *Beyond the door,*
>   *There's peace, I'm sure.*
> *And I know,*
> *There'll be no more tears*
>   *In heaven.*

Many people talked about Clapton's veiled song for days after the Grammys, but I'm sure not many knew what he really said. He was still searching for answers to his tragedy. What a great opportunity for a Christian to step into a conversation about that song and explain God's promise of life in Jesus Christ both here and in the hereafter.

Don't get caught in the trap of thinking that once you have begun a spiritual conversation, you must take it all the way to sharing the Gospel and that you must then get a decision. When your friend begins to open up, you might think, *Man, I've only got five minutes until my appointment. How am I going to get to the Gospel that quickly?* Relax, take the five minutes you have, and plant whatever spiritual seed you can. Then pick up the thread again later, or even ask your friend if you can get together afterwards so you can talk about the spiritual subject that has been raised.

My wife was talking to another woman about the Lord the other day, and they were both walking toward our house, about 500 yards away. How much of the Gospel can you get through in 500 yards? Later Deb said to me, "I was talking a mile a minute. I wanted to go around the block one more time just so I could keep going, but she had somewhere else to go."

My wife can talk fast, so she got the Gospel in and talked about Jesus Christ and about accepting Him as Savior. If you can talk that fast—and the other person can listen that fast—great! But if you can't, that's okay. Your unfinished discussion gives you a reason to bring it up again later.

Our family has lately been praying that another family we know will come to Christ. Deb went out for coffee with the mother one day to talk with her about the Lord, and when she came back from their time together I asked her, "How did it go?"

"I was so frustrated," she said. "I tried a hundred different ways to turn that conversation to spiritual topics, but she didn't want to talk about anything like that. All she wanted to do was drink coffee and talk about crafts." I thought, *See, crafts can be a detriment at times!*

Seriously though, there will be times when you have primed your courage and you're ready to share Christ *right now*—but your friend is not ready to listen right now. That is a time for patience, for God *will* bring about that perfect time to talk if you keep praying and listening. It just might not be the day or hour you had scheduled.

Roadblocks Along the Way

Strange as it may seem, we may reach a point in our relationships with non-Christians when we will be tempted to avoid talking about spiritual matters with them altogether. We may stop thinking about ways we can plant spiritual seeds. We might even quit praying for that person. If you find yourself heading that direction, you've probably hit one of several roadblocks.

The first roadblock is: *becoming more interested in the relationship than in your friend's soul.* This is easy to do—friendship evangelism without the evangelism. We all want to be accepted by other people, and once we are accepted we're careful to avoid anything that might jeopardize that relationship.

This is especially true when as Christians we are accepted by people in "the world." We figure if they like us even though we are "religious," we have really arrived. At that point you have to ask yourself, "Why did I initiate this relationship in the first place?" You made that friend because you were concerned about his or her eternal soul. Don't become so cool in your friend's eyes that sharing the friendship becomes more important than sharing the truth.

Recall Jesus' words to His disciples on the evening before He was crucified: "If you belonged to the world, it would love you as its own. As it is, you do not belong to the world, but I have chosen you out of the world. That is why the world hates you. Remember the words I spoke to you: 'No servant is greater than his master.' If they persecuted me, they will persecute you also. If they obeyed my teaching, they will obey yours also" (John 15:19-20). Of course we don't want to force people to hate us, but we don't want to back off from our ultimate purpose in the friendship just so things will remain comfortable either.

I spoke to a Christian man not long ago who had worked for the same company at the same location for thirty-three years. "Have you ever had any opportunities to share your faith?" I asked him.

"Oh yes, all the time," he said.

That caught my attention, so I eagerly pumped him. "Just how did you share your faith with your coworkers?" He had worked with some of the same people for the whole thirty-three years!

"I lived the Christian life."

"That's great! And in those thirty-three years, what did you actually *say* to them about Jesus?"

"Well, nothing really."

"Let me understand this. In thirty-three years no one ever came up to you and said, 'I've noticed that you live an exemplary life, and I'd like to know why you are so different,' and therefore no one ever actually heard the Gospel?"

"Uhhh . . . that's right."

That conversation is unforgettable, not because I was critical of the man's silence, but because I wondered if I had been just as silent with friends and neighbors whom I had known for years . . . for decades. I had to ask myself a tough question: Was I more comfortable with their friendship than I was uncomfortable with their lostness? Maybe you should ask yourself that question too.

The following poem was found in the locker of an elderly lady who had died in the geriatric ward of a London hospital. The staff had thought she was senile and incapable of writing.

What do you see, nurses, what do you see?
  What are you thinking when you look at me?
A crabby old woman, not very wise,
  Uncertain of habit with faraway eyes.
Who dribbles her food and makes no reply,
  When you say in a loud voice, "I do wish you'd try!"
I'll tell you who I am as I sit here so still,
  As I rise at your bidding, as I eat at your will.
I'm a small child of ten with a father and mother,
  Brothers and sister who love one another;
A bride soon at twenty my heart gives a leap
  Remembering the vows that I promised to keep;
At twenty-five now I have young of my own
  Who need me to build a secure happy home;
At fifty once more babies play round my knee;
  Again we know children, my loved one and me;
Dark days are upon me, my husband is dead.
  I look to the future; I shudder with dread.
My young are all busy rearing young of their own,
  And I think of the years and the love that I've known.
I'm an old woman now and Nature is cruel.
  'Tis her jest to make old age look like a fool.
The body it crumbles, grace and vigor depart.
  There is now a stone where I once had a heart.
But inside this old carcass a young girl still dwells,
  And now and again my battered heart swells.
I remember the joys, I remember the pain,
  And I'm loving and living all over again.
And I think of the years all too few—gone too fast
  And accept the stark fact that nothing will last.
So open your eyes, nurses, open and see,
  Not a crabby old woman, look closer—see me!

That's touching, isn't it? It's amazing how we can look at people and assume so much . . . and forget so much. What do you see more clearly when you look at your non-Christian friend—a friend or a non-Christian? We must always be diligent to see *both*.

A second possible roadblock is: *taking offense at your friend's initial lack of interest and then rejecting him.*

Here's where we have to be patient and demonstrate Christian maturity and character. Our Lord was rejected too, remember? But Jesus' invitation was always open: "Come to me, all you who are weary and burdened, and I will give you rest. Take my yoke upon you and learn from me, for I am gentle and humble in heart, and you will find rest for your souls" (Matthew 11:28-29). Your non-Christian friend is worth your patience.

A Christian TV news anchorman in my home church was interviewed by my pastor one Sunday morning, and the pastor asked him to give his personal testimony of how he came to Christ. The newsman said that before he came to Christ he was intentionally mean to Christians who talked to him about the Lord. He'd say, "Don't talk to me about that garbage. I don't need your God," though he knew that deep inside he was searching desperately for answers to the questions plaguing his life. He was addicted to alcohol and had a four-pack-a-day smoking habit, but he kept others from seeing how needy he felt. He was actually very interested in what God could do to erase the pain in his life, though he wouldn't admit it. Don't give up on such a person; be mature enough to deal with initial rejection, understanding that beneath the person's thorny armor is an empty heart that only God can fill.

Sometimes a friend's rejection even turns into outright antagonism. The eighteenth-century French skeptic Voltaire once said, "In twenty years Christianity will be no more. My single hand shall destroy the edifice it took twelve apostles to rear." Yet as Voltaire's doctor cared for him on his deathbed in 1778, he was astounded at the torment in Voltaire's soul. At one point Voltaire cried out, "I am abandoned by God and by men." Just before he died he shouted, "My feet! My feet! They're on fire!" Sooner or later your friend's antagonism toward the Gospel will shatter in the face of the realities of life and death. Be there to help him pick up the pieces by sharing the Good News with him.

A third roadblock is: *watering down the Gospel for the sake of the relationship.*

I'd love to tell all my non-Christian friends, "God loves you and has a wonderful plan for your life," then stop right there. I'd rather not have to explain to my friend that he, like all people, is a sinner who must accept God's free gift of eternal life in Christ. But our friends must understand that *their* sin made Christ's sacrifice absolutely necessary.

We tend to classify sinners. Here's a "nice sinner" over here, and there's a "really bad sinner" over there. Some of the friends to whom you are building bridges may be very nice sinners. They're pleasant; they're funny; they're kind. However, all of us can trace our spiritual roots back to the Garden of Eden and to the sin of our original father and mother, Adam and Eve. We all bear the burden of sin as members of the human race, even though some of us may not manifest our evil nature as obviously as others. We all need to understand and accept the whole Gospel message—our sinfulness and Christ's death to bring us forgiveness—to be saved.

Russian writer and activist Alexander Solzhenitsyn has cited our universal sinfulness: "If only there were evil people somewhere insidiously committing evil deeds, and it were necessary only to separate them from the rest of us and destroy them. But the line dividing good and evil cuts through the heart of every human being. And who is willing to destroy a piece of his own heart?" It is hard for some people to look in the mirror and admit they are sinners in need of a Savior. You, as a Christian friend, need to become their spiritual mirror so they can see themselves as they really are.

Keith and Robert had been best friends since they were high school freshmen. They loved books, showing off in class, and bad puns. They went through high school in the same church, attended the same youth group, and sang the same choruses. Robert had been there when Keith was baptized. Even though they went through rocky times, as all friendships do, Robert knew their common faith would always be the glue that held them together.

After the first months apart from each other during their freshman year at different colleges, they met again to catch up on what had been happening in their lives. Both had changed, but Robert had not anticipated how much.

"I want to tell you something," Keith said to Robert as they rode through town in Keith's rattling car, "but I don't know how to say it." Finally it poured out. "I'm gay," Keith admitted. "Do you want me to pull over and let you out?" he probed cautiously.

"Why?" Robert smiled.

"You don't mind being seen with a fag?" Keith asked.

"You're still my friend, Keith. Being gay doesn't change that. But you can probably guess how I feel about it."

"That it's a sin."

"Yes, but . . ." As Robert and Keith talked more, it became evident that Keith had never really asked Jesus Christ to be his Savior.

"Three years ago I became a Christian," Robert continued. "I don't want this to sound like a sermon, but being a Christian has really meant something to me. God has changed me. I'm only sorry I haven't talked with you more about it before now. Ever since I became a Christian, I know He hears my prayers, know my hopes, and guides me. God can do the same thing for you."

Keith's silence said it all. Robert had to make one more point though.

"Even though I do believe homosexuality is a sin, I don't think God views it differently than any other sin. The results are the same—a broken relationship with God and with other people. But the good news is that God is willing to forgive and heal people, no matter what they've done. All you have to do is ask."

"Uh huh," Keith mumbled.

Silence. Then Keith took a deep breath and said, "So, are you dating anybody?"

"No," Robert said quietly.

"Have you ever wondered what it's like to love another man?"

"No . . . never."

That was Robert and Keith's last time together as true friends. They saw each other occasionally in the next couple of years, and then they just lost track of each other.

Reflecting on their last time together, Robert says, "I regret the loss of Keith's friendship, and I wonder sometimes how I would act if I had the chance to relive that conversation. Because the truth of the Gospel has not changed, I think I'd lose Keith all over again. Some people might say that would be my problem, not Keith's. Perhaps. It's true that I'm not comfortable spreading a watered-down Gospel that never mentions our need for God's love and forgiveness. And I'm not a good enough actor to pretend that life apart from God is as right as a life of belief. Had I been able to do those things, I might have held on to my friend. But I would have sacrificed my Savior."

We want to reach out to people, but not so far that we lose hold of the very Gospel we want to share with them. I think the apostle Paul understood that better than most of us when he said, "For we are to God the aroma of Christ among those who are being saved and those who are perishing. To the one we are the smell of death; to the other, the fragrance of life. And who is equal to such a task?" (2 Corinthians 2:15-16). Paul knew that the Gospel he preached carried the smell of salvation and life to those who accepted it . . . and the stench of death and judgment to those who didn't. The Gospel didn't vary; truth can't change and remain the truth. Not everyone we befriend for Christ will ultimately accept Him, but there is no other way in God's plan to bring them into the family of faith.

A fourth possible roadblock is: *downplaying your own enthusiasm about Jesus.* I have been learning about this one recently. I usually am very sensitive about how I come across to other people, but I think I had become a bit too careful. For example, when I'm playing tennis and get excited about a good shot, the first thing that comes out of my mouth is usually "Praise the Lord" or something like that. I was curbing that response when I was around my non-Christian friends, and I had to remind myself that I don't need to do that. When my friends know I am a follower of Jesus Christ, I also want them to know that I don't talk about Him only on Sunday. I take the Lord with me into my week. I talk about Him all the time. I want friends to hear me say, "I thank God for doing this for my family," or "I praise the Lord that He protected me and got me out of that dangerous situation," or "Ken, I'm asking the Lord to heal your knee." I don't do this so much that I get obnoxious, but I do want to make it clear to them that the Lord is present and working in my life every day.

More than enough people today walk around with long, sad faces that reveal their empty, sad hearts. Unfortunately, too many of them are Christians. Why not have a smile on our face because the Lord is in our life? Why not have praise for God on our lips for His many, many blessings that we continue to discover day by day?

In a world that's looking for happiness, we can beam like light-houses that show the way to safety in the storm. Let your enthusi-asm shine!

A fifth roadblock is: *being critical of your friend's behavior or lifestyle.* A woman who had come out of the drug culture when she accepted Jesus Christ as her Savior told me that all her friends were still using drugs and the Christians in her church encouraged her to break off relationships with them. "But I really wanted those people to come to the Lord like I had come to the Lord," she said.

It would have been easy for her to back away from her non-Christian friends and to criticize the lifestyle she had just aban-doned, but instead she kept going to the drug parties where her friends hung out. Everyone there was high except her, and she spent the whole time talking to people and praying for them. Eventually she led one of her friends to Christ, and then that woman's husband—the drug dealer for the whole group—came to Christ also!

"I'm so grateful I didn't pull back from them," she said later. "Nobody could go to their parties and just walk in. Who was going to reach my friends for Christ?" I'm certain her drug-abusing-now-Christian friends are glad she didn't pull back too.

I later met this friend who had come to know Christ. Both women beamed with the love of Jesus, and both had a zeal to share that love.

A sixth roadblock is: *forgetting that we may not be the only one building a bridge to them.* Our family has been praying for another couple on our block to come to Christ for some time now. As we have gotten to know them, we have discovered how tough they are and how indifferent they are to the Gospel message.

I was speaking in a church in another town when afterwards

a couple came up to me and asked if I happened to know some friends of theirs that might live very close to my home. In fact, their friends were indeed the "tough" couple on our block! "I pray for them every day," this Christian woman said. "The wife was my best friend in high school and all through college. We'd like nothing better than to see them come to the Lord." It never occurred to me that the tough couple I had been praying for might also have other Christian influences in their lives. You may not be the only one sowing spiritual seed in the lives of your non-Christian friends. As I said before, actively pray for other Christians to enter the lives of the people you are befriending.

Friendship evangelism is both friendship and evangelism. We have been concentrating mostly on the friendship aspect up to this point, but remember that this friendship is leading somewhere. Friendships have a purpose—that of sharing the good news of the Gospel. If you keep that ultimate goal in view, you can more easily focus your activities toward that end. And if you keep that purpose in mind, you will become much more sensitive to those moments when the door swings open in your relationship and you are given an opportunity to talk with your friend about God, Christ, and eternity.

9

Making Sure Your Words Communicate

MANUFACTURERS POUR BILLIONS OF DOLLARS INTO ADVERTISING every year. When they promote their products in international markets, you'd think they'd be careful how their ads translate into another language. Sometimes they aren't, however, resulting in a promotional nightmare for them—and cheap laughs for us! For example:

- When Clairol exported its new Mist Stick to Germany, the company did not realize that in German "mist" is slang for "manure." Not many German women wanted to curl their hair with a "manure stick"!

- Chevrolet tried unsuccessfully to market its Nova model in Spanish-speaking countries, not knowing that "nova" means "does not go" in Spanish.

- Coors beer used the slogan "Turn it loose!" in their ad campaigns, but in Spanish the slogan read "Suffer from diarrhea!"

- Pepsi adopted the phrase "Pepsi brings you back to life" to advertise its soft drink, but in China it was translated "Pepsi brings your ancestors back from the dead." Has Pepsi discovered the fountain of youth?

We chuckle at those blunders, but no doubt they confused customers internationally. You probably wouldn't chuckle at all if I told you that we Christians commit the same kinds of confusing blunders when we try to communicate the Gospel to non-Christians. We may speak the same language as our friends, but our words may not communicate the message we intended.

An article in the *New York Times* featured sayings from church signs around the country. Many of the sayings were meant to be evangelistic. One pastor explained, "We look upon it as an opportunity twenty-four hours a day, seven days a week, to have the truth of the Christian faith flashed up for all of the passers-by." Here are a few examples:

In order to get to Hell you have to step over Jesus.

Free faith lifts every Sunday.

Let Jesus fix your achy breaky heart.

Heaven's directions: Turn right, go straight.

I know all these messages were well-intentioned, but how much do they communicate about the eternal truths of the Gospel? What would the person who read them really understand?

When I was in college, a professor in one of my college classes challenged us, "Take these words on the board and explain what they mean so the average person on the street would understand them." He had written words like "sin," "redemption," "faith," and "born again"—words we often use when we share Christ with somebody else.

It was one of the best assignments I've ever had, because I

realized that I was using Christian jargon without thinking about whether or not the person to whom I was talking understood it.

Have you ever heard computer programmers talk to one another? They are the most fascinating people in the world, but you don't want to get into a conversation with them. Why? Because soon they start talking "computerese," and it all goes right over your head. You can't possibly understand it, but they know what they are talking about because they live and work in their computer world.

Most non-Christians don't live or work in our Christian world. We may think we are communicating to them when we use Christian terminology, but most of the time they don't have a clue what we are saying. "I told my friend that if he would lay down his burdens and be justified by faith in Christ, he'd be redeemed." "Your iniquities are your real problem. You just need to be washed in the blood of the Lamb." There's no way they can grasp what we are saying if we use language like that!

A man once said to me, "I wish my pastor would just talk like a normal person." I am a minister, so I can tell you truthfully how frustrated I feel when Gospel ministers talk over people's heads. Jesus talked in the common language of His day. He used stories and illustrations to make His message clear. Why don't we do that?

Before we begin to talk about using your personal testimony of faith in Jesus Christ as a tool to communicate with your non-Christian friends, I'm going to give you the same quiz my professor gave me those many years ago. Before you look at the answers below, define the following terms as simply as you can—so even your non-Christian friends would understand them: *saved, born again, sin, faith, repentance, receive Christ, lost, eternal life.* Now compare your answers with the definitions given below.

Saved	To be rescued.
Born again	Spiritual birth; renewal; to come alive spiritually.
Sin	Living independently of God; crime against God's law.
Faith	Trust; reliance.
Repentance	To turn around; to change your mind; to turn to God.
Receive Christ	To place your trust in Jesus for forgiveness and heaven.
Lost	Separated spiritually from God.
Eternal life	Life that never ends; life with God and others forever.

Please understand that my definitions are not perfect, though I have found them helpful as I have attempted to make my witness for Christ more understandable. If you think you have discovered some better definitions, I'd love to hear them! Send them to me, please. We can help each other be as effective in our witness as possible.

In 1993 a car carrying four women became stuck on the railroad tracks in Industry, California, as the driver tried to steer it around the lowered crossing arm. The women rolled up their windows and locked their doors as a would-be rescuer pounded on the car to warn them of the train bearing down on them. Eventually he broke into the car and pulled three of the women to safety, but the oncoming train plowed into the car, engulfing it in flames and killing the fourth woman before she could be rescued. Interviewed later, the three survivors explained that they thought their rescuer was trying to rob them, and they panicked. The women were recent immigrants who did not understand what the man was saying.

As we talk to people about the eternal disaster they can avoid by trusting Christ as their Savior, let's make sure we are speaking their language, because we too are trying to rescue people from certain death.

Using Your Testimony

My dad was the last in our family to become a Christian. Raised Roman Catholic, he had many misconceptions about God. He figured he could work his way to heaven. My sisters and I prayed he would one day come to Jesus so we could all go to church as a family, like the others in our church.

When Dad was sixteen, he married Mom—and never even finished the tenth grade. He was baptized in Mom's church—he figured that was good for family relations. But neither he nor Mom had a personal relationship with Jesus Christ at that time.

Dad worked construction, provided for his family, and tried to do the right thing for us kids. But even after my sisters, Mom, and I accepted Jesus and attended church each week, Dad did no more than drop us off at the church's front door.

Dad figured he didn't need to sit in on any sermons—after all, he helped fix up the pastor's house and helped out around the church with his carpentry skills. In fact, Dad was mowing the church lawn one Saturday when he really started thinking about life, love, and his need for direction.

My dad's dad had been a stern father. No love. Few words of encouragement. Dad hoped to gain his father's approval by doing a good job on whatever he was asked to do.

As he mowed that day, Dad thought about how he was much the same dad to his kids as his father had been to him. How could he be a better father? he wondered.

And in many ways, he realized, he had the same relationship with God too—distant, dependent on doing a good job. He also knew, from sermons he'd heard in Mom's church years ago, that God offered a lot more.

Turning off the mower, Dad decided to take a break. Coffee in hand, he wandered into the sanctuary and up to the Lord's Table, where a Bible lay open to Romans. He read, "Therefore, since we have been justified through faith, we have peace with God through our Lord Jesus Christ" (Romans 5:1).

"Through faith"? Dad thought about that. His mowing the church lawn didn't count for anything. "Peace with God"? He knew he didn't have that.

In the silence of that empty church, Dad surrendered his life to Jesus Christ.

The change in his life was dramatic. He had tried to quit smoking for years, and we had tried to scare him into it by putting articles about the dangers of smoking under his pillow. Nothing worked though. But that day he stopped smoking—immediately. He has never picked up a cigarette again. The next Sunday, the whole family piled into the car and off we went to church. And at his job, Dad took out his New Testament at every break.

Dad worked with some rough characters at his construction job. But it wasn't long after he came to Christ that his coworkers noticed a change, and they began to ask him what had happened. He would sit on a pile of two-by-fours, share his story, and see person after person come to Christ right there at the construction site. One of them is now a missionary.

My dad would be the first to admit he is not well-educated. He isn't eloquent, and he didn't know a lot of Bible verses. But he did have his personal story. That was enough for those he led to Christ.

I asked him once, "Dad, how many people have you led to the Lord?" In the back of his Bible he has written the names of ninety-two people who have trusted Christ over the years after he shared his testimony and the Gospel.

Dad is still quick to talk to people about the Lord. He told me once about an elderly man in his neighborhood who used to be a tremendous golfer. The man actually had a picture of himself and Arnold Palmer in a tournament together—the man had beaten Palmer that day! That man didn't golf so well anymore, but after learning my dad golfed some, he said, "I'll teach you to golf a little better, if you want." They began talking, and Dad said to me later, "I had the greatest opportunity to sit down on the front lawn and explain the Good News of Jesus Christ with this man."

I asked Dad, "What did you talk about? How did you approach it?" Dad said he simply used his personal testimony. Here's my Dad, fifty-nine years old at the time, still thinking about people who need to come to Jesus Christ and using what works for him—his story. Why not? For him, coming to Christ was a life-changing experience.

Each of us can tell our story of when we came to Christ, and it's important to use that story if we can. You may be saying right now, "I haven't had a rough background like your dad, Dan. I didn't do drugs either. I wasn't a fugitive from the law. I came to the Lord when I was very young."

It's interesting to me that my mom doesn't use her testimony very much because it's not nearly as dramatic as Dad's. Similarly, my wife was brought up in a Christian home and came to Christ when she was eight years old. She can't very well say, "I used to be a horrible person. I stole crayons from the 2s and 3s department at church." So what does she do? She talks about the here and now. What is God doing in her life these days? How is God helping her raise her children? How does God help her put up with her husband, who can be a real pain at times? Start with your life now if you think your past is not spine-tingling enough to use as your testimony.

Is Jesus real in your life? You can't tell others about Him if you have no relationship with Him. What difference does He make for you?

Even if you want to include a past conversion experience in your testimony, it might be more effective to share what Jesus Christ is doing in your life right now. This is especially true if you are sharing your testimony in response to a felt need that you have perceived in your non-Christian friend. If you can communicate that trusting Christ was not only an experience "way back then," but that it has become a vital, daily relationship in your life, your friend may realize more clearly that Jesus' power is available *right now* to cleanse sin, to heal hurts, and to give real life. However, this assumes that you actually have a vital, growing relationship with Jesus Christ today. If your Christian walk is stagnant . . . if you worship Him only one hour a week on Sunday morning . . . if you don't feel the need to regularly study His Word and communicate with Him through personal prayer, don't fake it. Rebuild your relationship with Him as you reach out to build relationships with others for His sake.

The Power of Your Story

Your testimony can be powerful and persuasive, and there are four reasons why. First, *it's personal.* It's something that has happened *to you.* So just tell the story. You don't have to memorize fifty Bible verses; you don't have to be afraid of mixing up the points in your Gospel presentation. Your story is very non-threatening to the person listening to you.

Do you remember the famous encounter that Jesus had with

the Samaritan woman at the well (John 4)? She had two strikes against her in that culture. First, she was a woman; second, she'd previously had five husbands, and the man with whom she was living at that time was not her husband (verse 18). Yet when she perceived that Jesus was a prophet (verse 19) and then understood that He was the promised Messiah of God (verses 25-26, 29), it was the personal nature of her testimony that made others within her city curious about hearing the Lord too. "Then, leaving her water jar, the woman went back to the town and said to the people, 'Come, see a man who told me everything I ever did. Could this be the Christ?' . . . Many of the Samaritans from that town believed in him because of the woman's testimony, 'He told me everything I ever did'" (verses 28-29, 39). She simply told what God had done for her personally, and people listened and believed.

Second, *your testimony is conversational.* When your non-Christian friend listens to your story, it isn't like he's sitting in church listening to a sermon. He may be at your kitchen table with a cup of coffee, just relaxing and visiting with you. He can stop you and ask questions; there can be give and take in your dialogue as you tell what God has done in your life. You don't need a soapbox, a microphone, or a pulpit. It's just you and the other person in a conversation.

Third, *no one can dispute it.* How can anyone argue that what you are saying about yourself didn't really happen? No one! If you have joy and peace and love in your life as a result of knowing Christ, that will be evident, and people will notice.

My dad was a hard-driving, irritable, quick-tempered person before he came to Christ. But God began to work in his life, and the people he worked with could see it. That's why they came to him to ask about it. They could see his personality was changing, and they wanted to know why.

Do you remember what happened when Jesus healed the man who had been blind since birth (John 9)? The Pharisees were upset because Jesus had healed the man on the Sabbath, so they interrogated him, then his parents.

"Is this your son? Is this the one you say was born blind? How is it that now he can see?"

"We know he is our son, and we know he was born blind. But how he can see now, or who opened his eyes, we don't know" (verses 19-21).

The Pharisees didn't get the answers they wanted, so they questioned the healed man again. "Give glory to God. We know this man is a sinner," they said.

"Whether he is a sinner or not, I don't know. One thing I do know. I was blind but now I see!" (verses 24-25).

What were the Pharisees going to say to this stubborn, sighted man? "You must be mistaken! You can't really see. It's all a trick!"? The evidence was irrefutable, and so is the evidence of your life.

Fourth, *your testimony is interesting.* It is natural for friends to want to know more about each other. You certainly should be taking the time to listen and absorb what your friend is saying, and he will likely do the same if you have set the example. Even if your friend is antagonistic to the Gospel, he may still be interested in why you are so naive to believe in someone named Jesus Christ who died almost 2,000 years ago!

Barbara Bush gave a speech several years ago—before she became First Lady—comparing herself to then First Lady Nancy Reagan. "Nancy Reagan adores her husband," Mrs. Bush said, "and I adore mine. She fights drugs. I fight illiteracy. She's wears a size three. So's my leg." Her quip illustrates that she was not at all apologetic about who she was, and you shouldn't be either. Don't be afraid to tell how God has worked out His miracle of salvation in your life.

Planning Your Testimony

So where do you begin as you write out your testimony? What do you include? What do you leave out? I think the apostle Paul gives us a classic example of what a testimony should be in Acts 26. Paul talked about "what my life was like before I met Christ" (Acts 26:4-11), "how I gave my life to Christ" (verses 12-18), and "how my life has been different since I met Christ" (verses 19-23).

In the first section, verses 4-11, Paul talked about how he used to persecute the Christians, pursuing them from city to city, locking them in prison, and casting his vote against them to put them to death. All of this was before he became a Christian, of course. Paul was strikingly honest when he gave his testimony, and you should be also. You don't need to go into embarrassing details, but you do need to be frank enough about your story so that those who hear it can compare the you back then with you right now.

In the second section, verses 12-18, Paul described his famous Damascus Road experience with Christ. He detailed what he was thinking, what he was saying, and what he was doing when he met the risen Christ face to face. Paul's confrontation with Christ was dramatic and sudden. Yours may have been also, or you might have made a more calm, thoughtful decision after a long period of examining Christ and His claims. Whichever it was, be honest and genuine and provide the relevant details. After all, this is when you received the gift of eternal life!

In the last section, verses 19-23, Paul related what had happened to him after Christ became his Savior. In short, he couldn't stop talking and preaching about Jesus wherever he went! What has happened to you since you became a Christian? What have you stopped doing? What have you started doing? How do you feel about your life now?

I'll give you a few guidelines about the specifics of your testimony, but first review these general tips about writing and presenting your testimony.

KEEP YOUR TESTIMONY SIMPLE.   Although the story of how you came to Christ might still be very exciting to you, even if it happened many years ago, please curb the temptation to extend it into a detailed, minute-by-minute account of your life from birth until your conversion. Keep it short. Your story needn't be complicated and strung out like a good whodunit novel with eight subplots that take hundreds of pages to tie together so the reader can understand the climax at the end. Most people can successfully concentrate on someone else talking for about ten minutes at a time. That should allow you plenty of time to give a summary of your story with adequate details.

POINT PEOPLE TO JESUS CHRIST.   This is your story, but your story has meaning only because Jesus Christ is part of it. After reading over Paul's words in Philippians 3 for years, I am still impressed with how he focuses his story on Jesus Christ:

> *If anyone else thinks he has reasons to put confidence in the flesh, I have more: circumcised on the eighth day, of the people of Israel, of the tribe of Benjamin, a Hebrew of Hebrews; in regard to the law, a Pharisee; as for zeal, persecuting the church; as for legalistic righteousness, faultless. But whatever was to my profit I now consider loss for the sake of Christ. What is more, I consider everything a loss compared to the sur-*

*passing greatness of knowing Christ Jesus my Lord, for whose
sake I have lost all things. I consider them rubbish, that I may
gain Christ.*

—*Verses 4-8*

IDENTIFY WHY YOU NEEDED CHRIST.   Your need drove you to the
One who could meet that need—Christ. Your need for love. Your
need for forgiveness. Your need for the assurance of heaven when
you die. If your non-Christian friend has the same felt need or
needs, you are telling him that you have been where he is. When
you make it clear that Jesus Christ was the answer to your need,
you are showing him what his next step must be.

CLEARLY EXPLAIN THE GOSPEL MESSAGE.   If you are going to
point the way to Jesus Christ, take pains to explain the Gospel
clearly and simply. This isn't as easy as it might seem at first. As you
present your testimony, it's easy to get caught up in the emotion
of reliving your life-changing story. It's also common to be just
plain nervous! I suggest a rehearsed Gospel presentation to keep
you from saying too much and to help you cover all the vital facts.
For your convenience, a simple and clear Gospel presentation is
covered in the next chapter.

SHARE SEVERAL KEY SCRIPTURE VERSES.   I have included several
key verses in the Gospel presentation in the next chapter, and I
believe they are among the clearest you can use. However, feel free
to include verses that were particularly meaningful to you when
you trusted Christ as your Savior. Better yet, if you are sensitive to
the felt needs of your Christian friend, you might want to begin
with a verse that addresses that specific need. If you really want to
be prepared, consider memorizing a key verse on a few topics that
are common felt needs—guilt, forgiveness, love, or fear, for exam-

ple. If you do that, however, try to select verses that will point to Jesus Christ and lead into the main Gospel presentation. Whatever you do here, keep it simple.

AVOID USING ABSTRACT CHRISTIAN TERMS.   This is what I talked about at the beginning of the chapter, but I think it is worth mentioning again because it is so important. Have you ever seen a cross-section of an old water pipe that has become so choked by years of mineral deposits that it can barely carry a trickle of water? Every time you use a term that might not be familiar to your non-Christian friend, you are choking the flow of the Gospel message. Keep that communication pipe open between you and your friend by using terms that you both understand. The Holy Spirit can best use your presentation if you keep your audience in mind.

Recording Your Testimony

Get a pen and paper, find a quiet spot where you won't be disturbed, and begin to think back. What was your life like before you met Jesus Christ?

YOUR LIFE BEFORE CHRIST.   *Try to identify one problem or feeling with which you struggled.* I have found that many people come to the Lord because the person sharing with them had the same felt need as they do presently. What was going on in your life at that time, and how was that affecting your emotions and your disposition? Were you lonely? Empty? Searching? Did you have questions about life after death? Were you afraid of going to hell?

What was your attitude just prior to your exposure to the Gospel? This may have been different from your felt need. You may have felt empty, but you may have covered that emptiness with a selfish, arrogant attitude. You may have been lonely, but you may have propped up your loneliness with a self-made, I-don't-need-anyone image.

Next, *when and how were you brought face-to-face with the Good News of Jesus Christ?* Where did you hear the Gospel? Was it through a friend? Was it in a church service? Were you reading something?

What was your initial response when you heard the Gospel? Were you curious? Convinced? Skeptical? Why did you react that way?

GIVING YOUR LIFE TO CHRIST.   Now that you have remembered what your life was like before you met Christ, think about that time when you made the decision to give your life to Christ.

What helped you decide that you needed the Savior? Why did you trust Christ this time though you hadn't trusted Him before?

Do you remember a specific verse from the Bible that spoke to your heart? Maybe you were reading or someone was speaking at that time. What did that verse (or those verses) say that caught your attention and made you act?

How did you actually receive Jesus Christ? Share enough details so the Gospel message will be clearly presented here. Where were you? Was anyone with you? How did you feel? What did you say? What did you understand was happening at that moment?

YOUR LIFE AFTER CHRIST.   Perhaps you've heard the saying, "If you was what you is, then you isn't." That's bad grammar but good theology. If a person is just the same now as he was before he trusted Christ as his Savior, he needs to ask whether he truly came to Christ. When Christ enters a life, He changes it—sometimes immediately, sometimes slowly. *What about you has changed since you came to Christ?* What has been going on in your life since then?

What were your first thoughts when you received Jesus Christ? Some people feel a tremendous burden lifted. Others just have the assurance that they finally did the right thing. What was your experience?

What impact did Jesus Christ make on the problems you were experiencing before you met Him? For instance, my dad stopped smoking the day he trusted Christ. This can be one of the most meaningful moments in sharing your testimony. Here is where you offer proof of what you have been saying to your friend. We all need Jesus Christ, and once we let Him into our lives, He changes us and makes us into new people.

Of course, you don't want to give the impression that all your problems vanished the minute you trusted Christ. Even as Christians, we are in transition, becoming more and more like Christ as we let Him have more and more of us. But there should be some tangible elements of your life that have changed since you trusted Christ, and sharing these will encourage others to want to know Him.

10

Presenting Jesus Christ— the Bridge

YEARS AGO EZRA KIMBALL, A SUNDAY SCHOOL TEACHER IN BOSTON, felt burdened to share the Gospel with a member of his class who worked as a shoe clerk. One day a nervous Kimball cornered the young man at the store and stumbled through the Gospel message. Kimball left feeling discouraged that the Lord couldn't use his weak attempt at witnessing. But later that day D.L. Moody trusted Jesus Christ as his Savior because Kimball had obeyed the Lord. Moody later became the foremost American evangelist of the nineteenth century.

God used Moody to awaken a heart for evangelism in Frederick D. Meyer, pastor of a small British church. Meyer later came to America on a speaking tour, and during a speech on a college campus J. Wilbur Chapman came to Christ. Chapman later consecrated his life to Christian service and followed in the steps of Moody.

Chapman then employed former baseball player turned YMCA clerk Billy Sunday to help him in evangelism. When Sunday held a revival in Charlotte, North Carolina, a group of men became so excited by those who turned to the Lord that they planned another outreach, bringing evangelist Mordecai Ham to town to preach. One evening when Ham gave the invitation, Billy Graham went forward and trusted Christ. And you know the rest of the story!

What an incredible spiritual heritage one man started 140 years ago by overcoming his fear, stepping out in faith, and sharing the Gospel. The implications of leading even one person to Christ are *eternal.*

We've talked about planning the bridge you will build into someone's life, gathering the tools to build that bridge, constructing it, laying down the road to the other side, and even using your personal salvation story as part of the process. After all that is accomplished, however, and the time has come to share the Gospel with your friend, what do you say? That's what we want to talk about in this final chapter.

You Have Good News!

Our society is addicted to news. Billions of dollars are spent every year trying to quench our incessant thirst to know what's going on in the world. It is sobering, however, to take a good look at the kind of news bombarding us every day.

First, there's *bad news.* One newsperson recently said, "The glorification of crime by excessive and detailed reporting in itself contributes to and creates more crime. It is crystal clear that the overwhelming emphasis on bad news greatly contributes to the climate of violence which characterizes this country today." A few years ago a computer analyst studied the headlines in popular newspapers across America. He discovered that the most used words in headlines were "cop," "kill," "judge," "death," and "slay."

There's also *weird news.* An article in the *San Jose Mercury*

News told the story of firemen who had to use wire cutters and pliers to free a woman . . . from her designer jeans!

Then there's *useful news*. I read a review about a book entitled *Everything That Men Know About Women*. I tracked down the book because I was intrigued with the title, but when I found it, all the pages were blank! It was all a joke (though it was useful news to me because now I don't feel like I am the only male who doesn't have a clue about the opposite sex).

What about *good news*? The apostle Paul said, "I am not ashamed of the gospel, because it is the power of God for the salvation of everyone who believes: first for the Jew, then for the Gentile" (Romans 1:16), and the word "gospel" literally means "good news." When you heard the Gospel message and eventually trusted Christ as your Savior, that was good news, wasn't it? Too often when we build bridges into people's lives and share our testimonies with them, we forget that we are giving them good news that they desperately need. God hasn't left us in this world to wander about aimlessly and wonder why we're here and where we are going. But life may feel that way to someone who hasn't yet been told the wonderful story of God's love for them in Jesus Christ.

Someone once said that when we ask for advice, we are usually just looking for an accomplice. That is, we are usually just looking for someone who will agree with us. The good news of the Gospel is much more than good advice. We didn't find it in an Ann Landers column. Romans 1:1 mentions "the gospel of God." This Gospel is God's story of how He has provided eternal life for sinful people who are heading for eternal death. That good news was enough to drive Paul to the farthest reaches of his known world, just so he could tell others about Christ. When you give the Gospel to a friend, remember that it is much more than advice that presents a possible solution to his temporal problem. The Gospel is God's truth and a necessary solution to man's eternal problem.

Presenting the Good News in a Direct Way

You are probably well aware of the content of the Gospel, but it's easy to become confused in the excitement of the moment when you are actually sharing it with someone else. That's why I suggest that you memorize this basic outline and use it as a starting point in your presentation. It is simple yet complete.

The Basic Facts of the Gospel

TRUTH #1: GOD'S PLAN—PEACE AND LIFE.   God loves you and wants you to fully experience the peace and life that only He can give. The Bible says, "For God so loved the world that he gave his one and only Son [Jesus Christ], that whoever believes in him shall not perish but have eternal life" (John 3:16).

TRUTH #2: HUMANITY'S PROBLEM—SEPARATION.   Being at peace with God is not automatic because human beings by nature are separated from God. The Bible says, "All have sinned and fall short of the glory of God" (Romans 3:23). Romans 6:23 adds, "The wages of sin is death, but the gift of God is eternal life in Christ Jesus our Lord." Humanity has tried to bridge this separation in many ways—without success.

I like to use the illustration of swimming across the Pacific Ocean from California to Hawaii to clarify this point. If you and I jumped in the ocean at San Francisco and began to swim toward Hawaii, you might make it farther than I would because you are a better swimmer and you are in better shape than I. But both of us would fail miserably in our attempts to reach Hawaii. In the same way, some of us may be better than others if we compare ourselves to others, but we are never good enough to meet God's requirement of perfect goodness. We all fail miserably.

TRUTH #3: GOD'S REMEDY—THE CROSS.   God's love bridges the gap of separation between God and humanity. When Jesus Christ died on the cross and rose from the grave, He paid the penalty for our sins. Jesus Christ says, "I am the way and the truth and the life. No one comes to the Father except through me" (John 14:6).

Every other religion in the world is spelled "d-o." Only Christianity is spelled "d-o-n-e." While on the cross Jesus Christ proclaimed, "It is finished!" (John 19:30), a phrase that was written across debts that had finally been paid.

TRUTH #4: OUR RESPONSE—RECEIVE JESUS CHRIST.   God invites us to respond to His love by crossing the bridge through trusting Jesus Christ. This means accepting Christ's death on the cross as payment for our sins and receiving Him as our Savior and Lord. The Bible says, "To all who received him [Jesus Christ], to those who believed in his name, he gave the right to become children of God" (John 1:12).

God invites us to repent (turn from our sins), receive Jesus Christ by faith into our heart and life, and follow Him in obedience as the Lord of our life.

A person who is receiving the Lord Jesus Christ into his or her life as Savior from sin and its penalty can pray something like this:

> O God, I know I am a sinner. Right now I repent and turn from my sins. I believe Jesus Christ died for my sins, rose from the grave, and is alive forever. I open the door of my

heart and life, receiving Jesus Christ as my Savior. I want to follow Him as Lord of my life. Thank You for saving me. Amen.

My Story

I would like to share my own testimony briefly, simply as one example of how God brings individuals to know the Savior. I've mentioned before that I came to Christ as a teenager, and one of the main reasons I did so was because of my profound fear of death. When I was a little boy, my mom nailed a familiar prayer to one of the walls in my room:

> *Now I lay me down to sleep.*
> *I pray the Lord my soul to keep.*
> *If I should die before I wake,*
> *I pray the Lord my soul to take.*

For years I thought about that one phrase, "If I should die before I wake," because I wasn't sure what would happen to me if I died before I woke up.

Mom was a Protestant, and Dad was a Catholic, but neither of them really knew the Lord as Savior, and we never went to church. Mom and Dad taught me there was a God, and they told me there was a heaven, but they never told me how to get to heaven.

One day when I was seven or eight years old I asked Mom, "If I die before I wake, how do I know I will go to heaven?" Mom (this was before she became a Christian) told me, "Dan, if your good deeds outweigh your bad ones, you will go to heaven when you die." I love my mom and always will, but that night she told me the wrong answer.

And strangely enough, I knew in my heart that she had given me the wrong answer. But I didn't know what the right answer was. So before I went to sleep every night, I'd cross my fingers and repeat, "God, I hope I go to heaven. I hope I go to heaven." For years I would wake up in the morning, and my fingers would still be crossed from the night before.

From the time I was a little boy until I was in high school, I was the "manger man" for our family. Every Christmas I was in charge of setting up our family's manger scene in our home. But I didn't have a clue what that scene was all about. Why were those angels hanging over that little baby? Why were the baby and his parents in a dirty stable? Couldn't they find a decent bed for the child? Why did they have to lay him in a manger? Year after year as I set out the pieces of that nativity scene before Christmas and then packed each piece away again after Christmas, I had no idea how important that story was to answering my questions about death and heaven.

A close encounter with death heightened my anxiety about the afterlife even more. I fell off a cliff, broke both arms, and had to be rescued by an ambulance. I honestly thought I was going to die.

When a Christian family in our neighborhood befriended us and then invited us to church, I finally learned the answers to the questions I had been asking for so long. I discovered that Jesus Christ came to this earth as God in the flesh, lived a sinless life, died for my sins and the sins of the world, rose from the dead, and went back to heaven to sit in glory at the right hand of His Father.

As I sat in church one Sunday morning after the preacher had given an invitation to come forward and receive Christ as Savior, I remember sweating and clenching the pew in front of me until my knuckles were white. I knew I needed to accept Christ, and I knew I needed to walk forward and talk to the preacher, but I was too embarrassed to get up. Then I distinctly remember letting go, and I firmly believe that I became a Christian at that point. What a relief that was!

I was still scared as I went forward and a sixty-eight-year-old church deacon, Jim Cauthem, met me at the front of the sanctuary. He went over the Gospel message with me and then led me in the same short prayer I gave you earlier in this chapter. From that time on, I never again awoke in the morning with my fingers crossed, hoping God would take me to heaven if I died. Now I *knew* I was going to heaven, because Jesus had forgiven me.

Presenting the Good News in an Indirect Way

The following methods (some of which we've covered before) are effective ways of exposing non-Christian friends to the Gospel message.

- Talking to God often about the people named on your prayer card.

- Developing relationships.

- Sharing your own story.

- Taking them with you to a church outreach.

- Inviting them to dinner and a crusade.

- Inviting their children to VBS or other children's programs.

- Giving them appropriate Christian materials such as books, magazines, or tracts.

Recently I taught this material as a seminar at a local church. Three hundred people attended the five-hour seminar on relational evangelism. What was so exciting was that the people planned a Thanksgiving outreach so they would have a reaping tool. Churches should evaluate all their programs and see if they are giving people the tools and the events to help their friends come to Christ.

When You Share the Good News

Compliment the person's honesty and his willingness to think about spiritual matters. A friend once told me he was talking about the Lord to someone who was very guarded about discussing it. But the non-Christian finally opened up when my friend kept affirming him for considering Christ at all.

Confess the doubts and struggles you had yourself when and since you received Jesus Christ. God may have taken certain bad habits out of your life immediately after you became a Christian, but you are probably still struggling in some areas of your life. Be honest. Life isn't rosy and perfect for most of us, even if we do know Christ as our Savior. But the difference for the Christian is that God promises to be there with us no matter what we go through.

Communicate at least one area of the Gospel that has significantly impacted you (perhaps love, forgiveness, assurance of heaven). I've heard people say they felt a huge weight lifted from their shoulders when they trusted in Christ. Forgiveness was important to them. Others have told me that they never realized how much God loved them. Review your written testimony if you need to, and remember what impressed you most when you finally trusted Christ.

Concentrate on winning the person, not on winning an argument. Your friendship should not end if he or she rejects the Gospel.

Someone once asked a woman what she did for a living, and she said, "I am a follower of Jesus Christ disguised as a waitress." You may be a stockbroker, a homemaker, a plumber, a teacher, a lawyer, or a computer programmer. But if you are truly a follower of Jesus Christ, your life has a purpose beyond your job, your activities, and even your family. God has placed you where you are right now because there is someone there to whom you can build a bridge for the sake of the Gospel message. Just remember, when you step out in faith, the Lord steps out with you.

Using Events to Share the Gospel

Let's be very honest about something. What if you build that relationship with your non-Christian friend, you share your testimony, you are sensitive to that person's felt needs, but you have a hard time getting to the point of actually sharing the Gospel as I have outlined it in this chapter? That's when inviting your friend to evangelistic activities becomes so important.

Be aware of events sponsored by your church or churches or ministries in your community where you know the Gospel will be presented. Evangelistic luncheons for business persons. Evangelistic campaigns in your area. Golf tournaments sponsored by local churches. Craft classes where women can bring their non-Christian friends to hear a short Christian testimony or Gospel presentation. Special holiday services at Christmas or Easter. What is going on in your community that you can use as a tool for the sake of the Gospel? Remember, your ultimate goal is to see your friend come to Christ. If you can invite that person to an event designed to present the Gospel, God can use that occasion just as effectively as if you presented the Gospel message yourself.

I came across a wonderful letter a while back that underscores the importance of inviting your friends to activities where the Gospel is given. It was sent to the offices of the Luis Palau Evangelistic Association after a campaign in Tulsa, Oklahoma.

Dear Luis Palau,

About three years ago I was diagnosed as having melanoma cancer and immediately underwent surgery to have it removed. A year later the cancer reared its ugly head and again surgery was required, but much more serious this time. About a month ago another malignancy was found, resulting in many tests to determine the best method of treatment.

Until this time I had considered myself a pretty tough guy, but with a gentle heart. I am a self-educated and somewhat self-made man working for a solid company with its corporate offices located here in the city.

Until recently I had fought all my own battles and thought I could continue to do so. At about this same time, right after the third tumor was discovered, I began to realize that help was needed, but I wasn't sure where to look or what to look for.

I began to hear about this evangelist who was coming to Tulsa. He had a very strange sounding last name, and to me it kind of sounded like a half-word.

As it turned out, our company was a sponsor for the Luis Palau Tuesday business luncheon, and I was invited. And what an important day in my life that was. That was the beginning of the journey for my wife and me.

Your illustration that God is not angry or disillusioned with us because God has no illusions about us came down on my head like a ton of bricks. A simple statement that I had never heard before, and yet it rings with such truth and strength.

> *October 12, 1994 at approximately 9:30 P.M. in the Maxwell Assembly Center in downtown Tulsa became the most important day in the lives of Jim and Marcia Payne On that night you, Dr. Luis Palau, invited us to take a short, but important walk down to the altar on the arena floor and commit our lives to our Lord and Savior Jesus Christ. We accepted the invitation and began our new journey. What a wonderful and glorious night! Marcia and I together receiving and committing our lives to Jesus Christ.*
>
> *When we arrived earlier that evening we were two. When we left, we were three—the Lord, Marcia, and Jim. What a team!*
>
> *Once again, we thank you for coming to Tulsa and helping not only us but thousands of others to find Jesus Christ. Thank you, Dr. Palau, and praise the Lord.*

This story moves me because Jim's journey to Christ began when a Christian businessman invited him to that evangelistic luncheon. I had a chance to talk to Jim later, and I learned that a relationship had been established between Jim and his Christian friend. Jim's friend had been there through all three of the cancers. He knew Jim's felt need. He had shared his life with Jim and planted spiritual seeds in Jim's life. But when he invited Jim to an evangelistic outreach, *then* Jim opened his life to Jesus Christ. Just as Philip invited Nathanael to meet the Lord whom he had found (John 1:43-51), you can invite your friends to "come and see" events designed to share the Gospel.

Reaching into the Darkness

In 1887 a twenty-one-year-old woman traveled to a home in Alabama to work with a small girl who could neither see nor hear due to an illness she had suffered. The deaf and dumb girl could only make unintelligible grunts and groans, and her bewildered and frightened parents had given up any hope that she would live a normal life. The little girl was Helen Keller, and her new teacher was young Anne Sullivan.

For weeks Anne used her fingers to spell words in the palm of Helen's limp hand, trying to teach Helen about words and language. Many times Helen's animal-like outbursts frustrated Anne to the point that she wanted to give up completely.

The breakthrough came on April 7 that year. As Anne pumped cold water from the well over one of Helen's hands, she simultaneously spelled *water* in Helen's other hand. For the first time the child understood that what she felt in one hand was related to what she felt in the other. Sixty years later Helen wrote about that incident: "Caught up in the first joy I had known since my illness, I reached out eagerly to Anne's ever ready hand, begging for new words to identify objects I touched."

As new light flooded Helen's dark world, it became apparent that she was brilliant. By the time she was ten years old she was writing letters in French to prominent European leaders. She mastered five foreign languages at a relatively young age. When Helen went off to Radcliffe College, Anne Sullivan was there beside her, spelling out in her hand the lectures in every class she took. Although Helen is still widely remembered for her amazing accomplishments, few people remember the name of her devoted teacher.

Anne Sullivan dedicated her life to one person, Helen Keller, so Helen could have a full life. I've thought about that sacrifice many times, and I always ask myself the same question: Am I willing to invest my life in one person so that person can have eternal life? I ask you that question too. Can you take the principles you have learned in this book and apply them to just one person who needs to know Christ? Will you reach into the darkness of a life without Christ and build a bridge?

Workers renovating the Washington Monument found nineteenth-century graffiti as they removed the marble wainscoting inside the landmark. An anonymous scribbler, known only by his initials—B.F.B., wrote: "Whoever is the human instrument under God in the conversion of one soul, erects a monument more lofty and enduring than this." In the sense that each individual soul God touches through us is eternal, that person was right. You may never have the names of ninety-two people whom you have led to Christ written in the back of your Bible like my dad does, and that's okay. But if I have convinced you that it is eternally worthwhile to invest your time, your prayer, and your resources to befriend just one person who needs to know Christ, I have succeeded. And so have you.

Now you have a decision to make. You can remain comfortable where you are. Or you can step out in faith and with God's help begin to build a bridge into the life of someone you know so that person will discover the bridge God has built to him or her. I would like to conclude by sharing this wonderful little parable by John Drescher (first published in *Discipleship Journal*), hoping it will help you make that very decision. I know it speaks to me as a follower of Jesus Christ about the necessity of actually fishing for souls, not just talking about it or planning for it. I hope it speaks to you too.

A Parable of Fishless Fishermen

Now it came to pass that a group existed who called themselves fishermen. And lo, many fish were in the waters all around. In fact, streams and lakes filled with fish surrounded the whole area. And the fish were hungry.

Week after week, month after month, and year after year these who called themselves fishermen met in meetings and talked about their call to fish, the abundance of fish, and how they might go about fishing.

Year after year they carefully defined what fishing means, defended fishing as an occupation, and declared that fishing is always to be a primary task of fishermen.

Continually they searched for new and better methods of fishing and for new and better definitions of fishing. Further, they said, "The fishing industry exists by fishing as fire exists by burning."

They sponsored special meetings called "Fishermen's Campaigns" and "The Month for Fishermen to Fish." They sponsored costly nationwide and worldwide congresses to discuss fishing and to promote fishing and hear about all the ways of fishing such as the new fishing equipment, fish calls, and whether any new bait was discovered.

These fishermen built large, beautiful buildings called "Fishing Headquarters." The plea was that everyone should be a fisherman and every fisherman should fish. One thing they didn't do, however; they didn't fish.

In addition to meeting regularly, they organized a board to send out fishermen to other places where there were many fish. All the fishermen seemed to agree that what was needed was a board that could challenge fishermen to be faithful in fishing. The board was formed by those who had the great vision and courage to speak about fishing, to define fishing, and to promote the idea of fishing in faraway streams and lakes where many other fish of different colors lived.

Also the board hired staffs and appointed committees and

held many meetings to define fishing, to defend fishing, and to decide what new streams should be thought about. But the staff and the committee members did not fish.

Large, elaborate, and expensive training centers were built whose original and primary purpose was to teach fishermen how to fish. Over the years courses were offered on the needs of fish, the nature of fish, where to find fish, the psychological reactions of fish, and how to approach and feed fish.

Those who taught had doctorates in fishology. But the teachers did not fish. They only taught fishing. Year after year, after tedious training, many were graduated and were given fishing licenses.

Some spent much study and travel to learn the history of fishing and to see faraway places where the founding fathers did great fishing in the centuries past. They lauded the faithful fishermen of years before who handed down the idea of fishing.

Further, the fishermen built large printing houses to publish fishing guides. Presses kept busy day and night to produce material solely devoted to fishing methods, equipment, and programs to arrange and to encourage meetings to talk about fishing. A speakers' bureau also scheduled special speakers on the subject of fishing.

Many who felt the call to be fishermen responded. They were commissioned and sent to fish. But like the fishermen back home, they never fished. Like the fishermen back home that engaged in all kinds of other occupations, they built power plants to pump water for fish and tractors to plow new waterways. They made all kinds of equipment to travel here and there to look at fish hatcheries.

Some also said they wanted to be part of the fishing party, but they felt called to furnish fishing equipment. Others felt their job was to relate to the fish in a good way so the fish would know the difference between good and bad fishermen. Others felt that simply letting the fish know they were nice, land-loving neighbors was enough.

After one stirring meeting on "The Necessity for Fishing," one young fellow left the meeting and went fishing. The next day he reported that he had caught two outstanding fish. He was honored for his excellent catch and scheduled to visit all the big meetings possible to tell how he did it. So he quit his fishing in order to have time to tell about the experience to the other fishermen. He was also placed on the Fishermen's General Board as a person having considerable experience.

Now it's true that many of the fishermen sacrificed and put up with all kinds of difficulties. Some lived near the water and bore the smell of dead fish every day. They received the ridicule of some who made fun of the fishermen's clubs and the fact that they claimed to be fishermen yet never fished.

They wondered about those who felt it was of little use to attend the weekly meetings to talk about fishing. After all, were they not following the Master who said, "Follow me, and I will make you fishers of men"?

Imagine how hurt some were when one day a person suggested that those who didn't catch fish were really not fishermen, no matter how much they claimed to be. Yet it did not sound correct.

Is a person a fisherman if year after year he never catches a fish? Is one following if he isn't fishing?

About the Author

Christianity Today profiled Dan Owens, associate evangelist of the Luis Palau Evangelistic Association, as one of fifty "Up & Comers"—one of "the many faithful disciples God has raised up to lead the church into the new millennium."

Since joining the Palau Association in May 1986 after serving for nine years on staff at two churches in California and Oregon, Dan has ministered in more than thirty nations, speaking to hundreds of thousands of people at evangelistic campaigns, youth rallies, colleges and universities, missions conferences, and men's retreats. As LPEA's director of training for evangelism and discipleship, Dan has crafted the Bridgebuilder relational evangelism training series that he teaches in preparation for citywide evangelistic crusades.

The British publication *Evangelism Today* says, "Dan Owens has a winsome way with words, and a smile that makes it possible to say almost anything without giving offense."

A fun, dynamic, and gifted communicator of a message that changes lives for eternity, Dan has been blessed with the gift of communication. Whether speaking to thousands of teenagers at a rally, college students at the university, or adults at a missions conference, Dan is at home in front of people.

A graduate of Christian Heritage College in San Diego, Dan also completed work on a Master's degree at Multnomah Biblical Seminary. Dan and Debby, married for eighteen years, have three sons.

Relational Evangelism Seminars

Dan Owens has presented the material in this book to thousands of people at seminars in churches and crusades throughout the United States and the English-speaking world. If you'd like a Relational Evangelism Seminar (entitled "Building Bridges for Eternity") at your church, call or write:

> *Dan Owens*
> *4650 N.W. Neskowin St.*
> *Portland, Oregon 97229*
> *Telephone: (503) 629-9888*